Paper, Poetry & Prose Volume VI

An Anthology
of Eighth Grade Writing

Students of
Pierce Middle School

iUniverse, Inc.
Bloomington

Paper, Poetry & Prose Volume VI
An Anthology of Eighth Grade Writing

iUniverse books may be ordered through booksellers or by contacting:

iUniverse
1663 Liberty Drive
Bloomington, IN 47403
www.iuniverse.com
1-800-Authors (1-800-288-4677)

Because of the dynamic nature of the Internet, any web addresses or links contained in this book may have changed since publication and may no longer be valid. The views expressed in this work are solely those of the author and do not necessarily reflect the views of the publisher, and the publisher hereby disclaims any responsibility for them.

Any people depicted in stock imagery provided by Thinkstock are models, and such images are being used for illustrative purposes only.

Certain stock imagery © Thinkstock.

ISBN: 978-1-4620-5212-7 (sc)
ISBN: 978-1-4620-5213-4 (e)

Printed in the United States of America

iUniverse rev. date: 8/29/2011

Lacrosse

By Anthony Ala

Fight
Insults, Slashing
Punching, Kicking, Tackling
Kids, Field, Ref, Coach
Yelling, Cheering, Bragging, Running
Clean, Fun
Peace

Lacrosse
Teeth are clenched,
Face as red as blood, taking a pose –
Striking the first blow.
Like a panther in the jungle, attacking back
The enemy falls, wincing in pain.
No more fear,
the fight is over.

Lacrosse
Running, Scoring
Shooting, Shouting, Passing
Clarkston, Waterford, Troy
Living, Joking, Shouting
Laughing, Playing
Fun

Brian's Cold Drink

By: Josh Alder

Game on. It was day one of my first ever salmon fishing trip. I was ecstatic to catch my first big salmon. I was also nervous because my dad's friend, Brian, kept telling me stories about how people have fallen in the river and been hurt when they were fishing. I eventually learned that he was kidding about ninety-five percent of the stories he told me, but I still kept them in the back of my mind.

After about two hours of sleep, I woke up with all the energy I needed. My dad and Brian were a little bit reluctant to get up but they managed to roll out of bed and get some breakfast. We got to the river at about seven in the morning. It was really cold but I didn't care! My excitement was too much to be concerned with being cold. I put on my waders and stepped into the river, with all the stories rolling through my mind that Brian had told me the day before.

After about an hour of walking, we had only caught one fish. We decided that we would walk to a deeper part of the river to see if there were any big fish over there. As we walked I noticed that the river was getting deeper and deeper quickly. I jumped on shore with my dad to make sure that no water got in my wadders, if it did it would make the whole trip cold and wet! Brian however, stayed in the river. I looked over from the shore and Brian was in about five and a half feet of water which meant that the water was close to spilling into his waders. All of the sudden I heard a loud, "Uhhhhhh!" As I turned to look all I could see was Brian trying to swim with the freezing water engulfing his whole body. He swam really slowly as all the water filled his waders. It was weighing him down.

He eventually made it to the shore and climbed very slowly up on the bank, and stood up without a word, you could tell he was so cold that he couldn't move. His face and lips were blue and numb. He didn't complain he just walked down the bank, and stepped back into the river. He fished with us for the rest of the day and then went back to the campground and changed his clothes. Even though it was only like five in the afternoon he built a fire and stood next to it for about four hours trying to warm up.

Broken Bones

By Ben Ancell

One day I was at my friend's house playing. I was on the swing set going really high up in the air. I went back almost parallel with the bar. Then suddenly I plummeted to the ground. I tried to brace the fall with my arm by basically punching the ground.

I am sure I heard a snap when I hit the ground. I was down for a while then I got up. I was crying because I hit hard, and my arm had snapped. (Which would not be uncommon for a ten year old boy to cry.) My friend's house was around the block from my house when this happened. I walked all the way back around the block to my house. Then my mom asked me what happened, so I told her and she tried to help me calm down. Then I had to wait almost two hours before my dad got home so we could go to Ambulatory.

I was in so much pain it was unbearable. Finally when my dad got there we left. We were sitting in the waiting room for a while then the lady called us back. I had an x-ray done to see the break in my arm. Then they splinted my arm with this cool thing that when it dry's it gets harder then stays that way. We put a sling on it to help hold it up. Then I went home with that for about a month.

Then a month later we went to a different doctor to get a real cast. I picked out blue for my cast. When the doctor was setting my bones I was in so much pain. I couldn't believe that he did not warn me that he was going to do that. It made me want to punch him out with my good hand! Then we went home, and about another month later I got a new cast.

When I got the first cast off my arm was extremely weak. I couldn't even move it was so weak. I was glad that it was healing though. My new cast I picked out orange for the new color. It was pretty cool the orange was a very bright color. I had about two more casts after that then a thing with a metal thing to hold my arm straight that one I could take off if I wanted to.

Butterflies

By: Kate Anderson

EW! Look at that thing flap it's disgusting, ugly, colorful wings! That's just plain out scary. AHH! Get away from me, AWAY!

What the-? What is this girl doing?! Maybe she's just stunned at how I'm so beautiful (Most likely). Why is she flapping' her arms like that anyways? And why is she running around in circles? All I know is that this girl has some very serious issues. Oh, I know. Maybe she's trying to fly?

EW! EW! EW! GET AWAY! AHH! Can't you hear my ear piercing screams!? PLEASE JUST GO AWAY! Wait… can Butterflies hear? I don't know. BUT JUST GO AWAY!

If this girl is trying to fly I swear, she is doing it so wrong! This girl is very, very, and I mean very, strange. And why is her mouth open like that? Seriously…

REALLY! GO AWAY! Here, I just put ten bucks on the ground here, take it and leave me alone. Aw! C'mon'. URGH!

Well sense this girl is, laying green things on the ground, opening her mouth, and running in circles… I'm just going to give her some air.

EUREKA! Finally! Yes! Wahoo! You're gone! Finally that ugly thing is gone and out of my life. Wait what's that?! NO! Not another one.

Remember the Clippers

By Megan Arandela

We'll be back together at Mott,
That's what all the teachers say.
But what if we didn't want to wait a year,
If we wanted Crary to stay?

So many things we'll never get to do,
So many things we'll never get to see.
But they just say it's good to try something new,
So, something new it'll be.

Yeah, for trying some new food or a new shirt,
Not an entire school!
We'll be at a brand new place for nine whole months,
'Cause the school board had majority rule.

Now there's only three short months
Before it's time to say farewell.
The days suddenly seem so short,
Only seconds 'til the very last bell.

Time flies by faster than before,
Life speeds up and hits you in a crash.
All you want to do is slow down
Comfort and familiarity disappearing in a flash.

So, sign some yearbooks, go say your goodbyes
And find some ways to feel better inside.
Ignore the feeling you'll never finish what you start,
That feeling you get when you're about to fall apart.

We all flooded straight out the door,
As the bell cries its final song.
Leaving behind the very place
Where we all belonged.

And now the never ending musical symphony,
The buzzing chatter, yells and laughter all gone.
The hallways and classrooms all still with silence,
But in the end the black and gold spirit lives on.

This is the school we'll never forget,
The place we'll always remember.
We are, and always will be
Crary Clippers! Forever!

Tears of Love

By Maria Arellano

Hello, anybody there?
Ummmmmmmm……..
I'm getting really scared in here!
Its really dark and spooky being alone!
I want to get out of here already!
I've been here for a bit more than nine months, look I just want to get out!
I'm so crowded, scrunched, and my legs hurt!
I can't even choose my own food to eat!
Give me a break, and let me out!
I can't wait to take my first breath and see the bright lights of the world!
Push mommy push!
Ouch not to hard, you're squeezing my shoulders!
That hurts!
Ahhhhhhhhhhhhhhhhhhhhhhhhhh……..
I'm almost out just a little more!
One more push and I'm free mommy!
Ewwwwwwwwwwwwwwww, what's all that gooey stuff all over me, its nasty!
Awwww is that mommy?
I got to stop crying, because I don't want mommy to think I'm a cry baby!

There is a tear of love coming down my cheeks and hers!
Mommy holds on tight, smiles, kisses me, and says," welcome to the world my darling baby".

Nowhere to be Found

By Anna Arthur

Lonely,
Where is she?
Not waiting when I come home.

Sitting by the door,
Scared, watching for me.
Why did she have to go?

She wasn't patient with us.
Not friendly with men.
Finally, biting dad.

Confused,
Why do I miss her everyday?
She is not at dinner.

She is not here.
Lonely.

Bullying

By Emily Balconi

Bullying somebody isn't right. Maybe that's why many teenagers commit suicide or runaway. The people, who bully, don't understand why they shouldn't do it. Even though they don't think bullying is right. Bullying is wrong and people shouldn't do it.

There are different ways to bully. Cyber bullying is when you're on the computer, and you say threatening things, or hurtful words to somebody when you know you're doing it. Pushing, shoving, hitting, and yelling at somebody, calling them names, and starting false rumors about somebody are also ways of bullying.

Many teenagers commit suicide because they are getting bullied. They think if they tell somebody, the bullying problem, will get worse. Some kids, who get bullied, don't go to school, or they drop out because they can't handle it anymore. That's why Michigan started the bullying program; so teenagers can be helped in school by knowing about bullying. The bullying program teaches teenagers that you shouldn't bully and if you see it you should stop it.

Most people bully because they think it's cool and fun, or they're just bored. It's not cool to push around, and call people names. Most people get bullied, because of what they are wearing, or what they look like. Who cares what they look like or what they are wearing? Teenagers come to school to get an education not to get bullied, and then end up dropping out.

People only bully because they're going through some things, or they take anger out on people by bullying. As you can see, that's why bullying is wrong!

My First Real Gig: Cradle the Fall

By Devin Baughn

It was an overly humid day. The slight breeze had that sharp bite that warned the coming fall. The sun had set and all older people had long since left the West Branch fair grounds. The small crowd that was left consisted of mostly teenagers and drinkers.

I was left to my thoughts in the small dressing room I was provided. It had a mirror, two dank flood lights, and an end table with a large lamp that was missing its shade. In the middle of the cobweb coated room was a large dusty arm chare that was an off white and dirty orange plaid design that aged it greatly. The seemingly constricting room had a distinct odor of old people and jello.

I had just finished inserting my false contacts that made my eyes appear to glow with the gold in the outline in the hourglass shaped iris. When I had my outfit finished all u could see is the gold shape outline of my eyes under my hood. My outfit was all black hoodie, V-neck, and skinny jeans. I did not recognize myself in the mirror as I walked out to meet the rest of the band.

I felt like I had white hot brand stuck to my stomach as I saw Augie outside my door. The previous band had finished its encore and proceeded to bow out. As the intermission swiftly ended and my cousin was don setting up the gear and hard wear. My heard was at my throat while my stomach was at my feet.

A slightly confused murmur followed my walking on the stage after Augie and that was followed by an enthusiastic roar as he introduced me. "Welcome tonight's featured singer from 'As We Are'" (this being my former band). The small sea of people seemed satisfied with the provided explanation. The bass erupted from the speakers starting the song that would warm up the crowd Metallica's "Whisky in the Jar". Soon enough the fans were chanting the letters "C- T- F" over and over. A strong voice that I did not recognize sprang from the bottom of my stomach as my lungs emptied and filled until the last note of the last song.

After the show I felt like a god. There wasn't a single word that found me for several minutes I was, by definition, speechless. It felt like the crowd of only around 200 was the only people in the whole world and they all looked up at me on the stage as we bowed out. I had finally obtained a fan base. No friends or even family was there to see me. I now had to totally different lives, back home I was a low life nobody but here I was above the rest. Yet Augie wasn't as eutectic as I was, he was to busy yelling at his guitarist telling him how bad he sucked it. But there is no feeling like the satisfaction of knowing that people are entertained because of you and you have created memories for people you will never meet.

Christmas Eve

By Alison Bednarz

Christmas Eve is by far my favorite day of the year. Its a day to get together with family you haven't seen in a long time. My mom's side of the family goes to my Great Grandma Bloom's townhouse to celebrate the holiday season. Family comes from all over the country just to meet up with everyone for this one night; at least sixty people go through her house that night. While some families may sit around and have a formal celebration my family definitely doesn't, we have many strange traditions that makes this night so much fun.

When people start to arrive, Grandma Bloom sends someone off to get Little Caesar's pizza. While we wait for the pizza we all snack on finger foods and catch with family we haven't seen in a while. After waiting the pizza finally arrives and we all jump up to get a plate. We say a prayer, then eat. Us kids usually go downstairs in Grandma Bloom's basement and sit around the ping pong table eating our pizza, jell-o, and pop while talking about what we hope to get for Christmas.

After everyone finishes eating we all rush up to her living room that's so small you have to fight over a seat. You look around and see people all over, on the floor, on the couch, on someone's lap, and most importantly... the chair. Everyone always fights over Grandma Bloom's huge recliner. When we all settle down we all face her

Christmas tree, most people may have a star on the top of their Christmas tree but Grandma Bloom doesn't. She has Scooby-Doo dressed up as an angel, eating pizza, in place of a star.

Before we start to open presents we all quiet down and listen to Grandma Bloom's directions. It's the same rule every year, you're not allowed to open your first present from Grandma Bloom until everyone gets their present. We have this rule because when my cousin was little she didn't get her first present until everybody had already opened theirs. Ever since then Grandma Bloom makes sure everyone has a present, even the adults, so no one would feel left out. After you get to open you first present my uncle passes out the rest of the presents. While we all open our presents Grandma Bloom sits and watches while setting all of her presents in a pile next to her, and when we're all done we watch her open her presents.

Christmas Eve isn't only about gifts, it's about family and all of our traditions. One way or another I hope that these traditions will carry on for many more generations, because in our family you always know that no matter where you live in the country you are always welcome at Grandma Bloom's for Christmas Eve.

My Weekend

By Brandon Behrendt

One winter weekend I went over to Michaels. Right when I got there we went outside. I forgot my coat at home so I was freezing the whole time. We walked about two miles in the cold to get to Arby's because we were hungry. When we got there we ordered our food and sat at a table and ate.

When we were done we started to walk back to Michael's house. It took about 30 minutes to get there. When we got there we decided we should have someone else come over. We said that we should call Tyler and see if he could hang out. So we did and he said he could. So we told Michaels dad and he said we could go get him in about 30 minutes. So we just went back outside and ran around his neighborhood.

When we got back it was 45 minutes later. His dad was mad and said we couldn't go get him because we got back late. So we just went inside and watched TV. After about 10 minutes his dad told us to call him and see if he still wanted to hang out. So we did and he said yeah. So we left to go and get him.

After we got back to from picking Tyler up we went up to Michaels room and played Dance Central. I was terrible at it but Michael, Tyler, and Michael's sister were good at it. After a while we just went to bed.

The next morning Michael's parents woke us up

to go downstairs and eat breakfast. Tyler and Michael walked out and went downstairs. I got up and fell off the top bunk and hit my head on the floor. After my head felt better I went downstairs and ate breakfast. When I finished my mom called me and said she was coming to pick me up. That ended my weekend.

A Scary Trip

By Tyler Bellant

I was riding my atv with my brother on this sunny morning. My family and I went on a trip to the U.P. for a vacation. My brother and I like to ride around on the street; we stay in a cabin when we go there. It was in the morning but sunny out. We live next to a lot of wooded areas by US. 2. So the woods were dark because they're so thick up north, which is surprising to be able to move through them.

My brother and I kept on seeing big black shadows down this one street. We ignored it for a while until I kept seeing them over and over. Finally, I told my brother to hold on and I'd be back. I rode down the street to see what it was. As I got closer it looked like dogs. So I got really close.

I looked and I saw a big black bear and two cubs with it! My brother turned and saw me blow by him at seventy mph, then he took off too.

When we got to our cabin my brother asked, "What did you see?"

"A mother bear and two cubs!" I replied.

He and I told my parents what I saw. They did not believe me. So, they drove to where I had seen the bears and there were prints left behind showing where they had been.

They said, "I guess you weren't lying after all!"

Hotel Key Card

By: Matthew Berlin

Once I went to a hotel; it was a great hotel. While I was there, I suddenly heard a loud voice, "I really like these hotel key cards! They're really cool!" It said.

I was some what flattered, that someone thought that I was cool! But still I was scared of what might happen to me later, notoriously people do not take good care of us – hotel keys that is! Suddenly this giant thing picked me up and slid me into a lock to unlock this huge door. I couldn't believe my eyes when the giant opened the door. It was like I just went to heaven! The room was gold everywhere; the gold letters over my eyes said, "Welcome" in English and a whole bunch more languages. Ok back to the room, it was AMAZING. So, there's one problem solved, now if I die I will at least be in an outstanding room.

The very next morning I heard a voice that sounded like a really loud yawn in women's voice.

Oh, it's just the giants' mom waking up. Her gentle hands just picked me up and next thing I know I am slipping into her pocket or at least someplace.

The kind women took me on a date for continental breakfast, but I just didn't get any of the breakfast.

Another day goes by and the giant kid picks me up and the next thing I know he throws me against the wall! But he said, "You Lieieieieieieieiei wooooooh Baaaammmmm oooowwwwwww!"

Ooohhh, man! I think I just broke my... well the past two hours where torturous!   Then, of course, I hear a loud voice saying, "You'd better find that card or you're in trouble! I am not paying $150.00 for a new one."

Another voice I have never heard before that came from a well dressed man and he said, "No problem, we will just let you off on this one so you don't have to worry about the card we'll just find it for you."

Hey wait! So you guys are just leaving me underneath this small crack and probably never see me again. Ok, that's alright I'll get used to it.

Inspiration

By Edward Birch

Inspiration is why people do anything. It keeps people busy. Inspiration is really what keeps you doing what you're doing. It is why people have created art, or written music, it is even why people invent machines.

Inspiration can come from anywhere at anytime. That is why an artist always has a pencil and sketch pad. It is why writers' always have notebooks, and why musicians always have a recorder, or something to work with. When you become inspired, you do what you are inspired to do.

When you feel it, you know. It just can't wait. You need to do what the inspiration tells you to. Different people get inspired different ways. Musicians and artist might be inspired by each others work, or someone else's. They could feel it from talking to certain people, or playing certain games. Maybe it just comes and goes.

Inspiration is why writing on demand is so hard for some people. Unless you feel it, you won't write. Drawing on demand, or painting on demand can't be done if you don't know what to paint or draw. If you're told to write a piece of music, you won't do it till you feel you have the inspiration and the idea. It's impossible to do anything without being inspired.

It is what makes the best music, or creates the best

art. Without inspiration, do you think Leonardo da Vinci would have painted the last supper in Milan? Without it, do you think Buddy Rich would have played the drums?   Or that Eddie Van Halen would be such a great guitarist? Do you think that any of your favorite television shows would be around if the creators weren't inspired in some way?

The Great Food Fight

By Timothy Blakely

Food. What does it do? What does it mean? Well, on one certain Friday, while I was wearing a brand new white t-shirt my mom had just gotten me, it meant trouble. I heard a lot of talk about an up coming food fight. But, it was just talk I wasn't really worried about it. When someone told me what we were having for lunch that day, it came to me. We were having sloppy joes as one meal choice and chicken nuggets and mashed potatoes for the second. It was the end of the year and I knew this would be "Food Fight Smash Out!"

It was perfect. Crary, my school, was closing down. It was the last day there, so we wanted to go out remembered! We did not care for any teacher that might get in our way because our minds were set on a great food fight.

It was second hour, I had lunch after third hour, when I over heard a few kids talking about how it was going to start. They had to get some kids to start throwing food and then someone would yell, "Food Fight!" But they had to get some people to start throwing food or nothing was going to happen. Eventually they got some people to go along with it – it seemed like the perfect plan! Or so I thought.

I looked up at the clock and saw that there was only ten minutes until lunch. I was getting nervous, kind of excited and my hands were sweating. I was thinking would I have the guts to throw food? Or will I wimp out like some of the others said they would? I had to consider the trouble I might get in. But, I couldn't get suspended I thought as the clocked ticked off the last thirty seconds of class. I was definitely rethinking my part of the plan.

BOOM! The bell rang for lunchtime, I heard kids racing down the hall. I can't wait for lunch, I was thinking. Soon I passed the raging crowd and got to my table. I didn't even take one bite before someone yelled, "Food Fight!" Immediately, everyone was throwing food! I saw a lunch lady try to stop the kids from throwing the food, and she was whacked with a full carton of milk. Suddenly the vice principal walked into the cafeteria – he was wacked in the face with a bun filled with barbeque sauce!

The entire food fight lasted about twenty minutes and five people got in trouble. It was fun!

Biking

By Jon Bloch

Biking
Awesome, Cool
Fun, Crazy, Experimenting
Jumps, Trails, Street, Park
Fun, Crazy, Fun, Crazy, Fun, Crazy
Very, Very fun!

Bike Parts
Frame
Wheels, Spokes, Hubs
Handlebars, Headset, Forks, Stem
Bottom bracket, Cranks, Chain wheel, Pedals, Chain
Tires, Tubes, Seat, Seat post, Grips
Bearings, Seat clamp
Bolts
The best thing about biking
is there is something new each day.

A Thunderstorm

By Katey Bowman

"Tweet,"
"Tweet,"
"Tweet,"
The birds sang.

The clouds blew away
the suns warmth,
cold water pounded
to the ground.

"Rumble!"
"Rumble!"
"Rumble!"
The thunder roared!

The clouds dumped
water, rain poured
down, soaking the
grass.

"Boom!"
"Pow!"
"Crack!"
The lightning shined,
it blazed into my eyes

"Crash!"
"Pop!"
"Crack!"
The ground shook as if an
earthquake rolled through.

"Snap!"
"Bam!"
"Boom!"
The thunder said,
as the dark storm
hissed by.

The sun's rays pushed
through the clouds,
and a glistening rainbow
appeared.

"Tweet,"
"Tweet,"
"Tweet,"
The birds sang.

Like 1, 2, 3

By Lauren Brill

Rachel Ruby Rood, I give my thanks to you,
For this unbreakable friendship we've been through.
We've been through a lot in the past year or so,
And things haven't gone how we planned them to go.
We were cut from the team,
It wasn't part of our dream.
They were a family to us,
But then it broke our trust.
We've sat and we've cried,
We were brave and we tried,
But most importantly, we've stuck together through
this hard time.
With you by my side, my tears seem to dry,
Together we grow stronger as time goes by.
We think back on the day that our hearts were taken
away,
We don't understand why it had to be this way.
We have felt disappointment, sadness and heartache,
But we will never give up or let our hearts break.
We struggle each day, locking the pain away,
We are there for each other – anytime, any day.
We are a team, you and me,
We could take on the world like 1, 2, 3.

Hunting

By Connor Campbell

Hunting, hunting, hunting
We grab our new gear
Ammo, hats, and shirts
Driving, driving, driving
We pull up to the house
Unpack, lay down, and stretch
Eating, eating, eating
We scarf down our breakfast
Gravy, biscuits, and eggs

Waiting, waiting, waiting
Waiting, waiting, yawn
Waiting, yawn, waiting
Napping, napping, zzzz
Waking, yawn, waking, stretch

Suddenly alert!
I see a deer
I
Slowly
Pull
My
Gun
Up
Breathe in

Breathe out
Crosshairs
Lined up…
POW!

I sit there for a moment in silence.
Wondering, wondering, wondering if I shot the deer.
Running, running, running I track down the deer.
Happy, happy, happy I have my very first deer!

Orchestra

By Alyssa Caples

Shaking, palms sweating, the waiting and anticipation have finally caught up with me after a month of preparation! Yet, I'm still so very nervous! The crowd starts to cheer me on. Then, they turn silent, waiting for us to start. My Instructor motions us to put our instruments up. Then we get the cue, and start playing.

Orchestra is very enjoyable to be in. All of the instruments are fun, but I play the cello. It is a lot of work, but gives you great satisfaction when you succeed. Personally, I love orchestra and thin it is great to be able to play an instrument. Different things are harder for different people. For some playing an instrument comes easy and naturally to them, to others it is a greater challenge and takes a lot of hard work ad concentration. For me, it's kind of in the middle, some of it comes easy and some I have to work hard to achieve.

Performing is the hardest part for me. Being in front of a huge audience makes me very nervous. My face turns as red as an apple, and after I start I shake horribly. I get so nervous that I mess up while I am playing. After I perform the clapping and cheering of the audience makes me feel happy and proud. I feel like I achieved something when I am finished playing.

Many people say, "Orchestra is stupid." Or,

"Orchestra is so lame, what's the point of orchestra?" Well, orchestra is very important in a lot of music. There are orchestra instruments in a lot of the popular music on the radio right now. Orchestra gives beautiful sound to those who enjoy it on cool, quiet nights.

Heartbreak

By Katelyn Chace

She's Beautiful
She's art work
She's hurting
She's heart broke
You hurt her bad but she loves you
You're begging her to say "I Do"
She's telling herself she will live, while she telling you
she will forgive.
He hurts her once more so she walks out the door
The car comes to a screeching halt
He blames himself; it's his fault.
As she is laid down to rest, he cries
"You were the best".

My First Flip Trick

By Chris Chalanda

On Saturday February, 19 I landed my first heel flip. It is the first trick on a skateboard I ever learned where you have to roll off your feet and off the board. I spent half a year learning it. I had my skateboard for two years. This is the day I land the heel flip.

In my garage I was practicing my ollie's. I started to ollie in control and I can ollie over curbs. After a couple of minutes I was going to do my kick flips, but I can't land them. I can get it to flip under my feet. So I've been working on it for a couple of mouths. Then after that I was going to work my heel flip.

Heel flips are like kick flips. I can flip them but I can't land them. So I kept working on them. Soon I started to land them on the very end of my heels. I was happy but it wasn't a real heel flip. One problem with the heel flip, you could flip the board right behind you.

I got really sweaty with so much practice, so went in my house to get some water. I came back into the garage, took a big breath and rode my board to the back of my garage. Then I jumped as high as I could, popped the board as hard, then rolled the side of my right foot off my board and landed it. "Some people think that a heel flip happens when you slide your heels off the board but it's not."

When I landed my first heel flip I was so excited! I

kept working on the landing most of the time. But when I'm having trouble, I keep on trying. Now, I land heel flips once in a while. After landing this it was cool to land my first kick flip one month later. I still struggle every time I try I don't jump high enough or pop enough. I'm still a beginner but I'll get better because of landing my first flip trick.

Crazy Day

By Youri Cho

When I was in kindergarten we did a Christmas Concert. The day of the concert I woke up late. My mom was trying to tickle me to wake me up, but no matter what she did I didn't wake up. Finally I woke up because she was just so annoying! But then I realized that I was so late! I had to run around to get ready. My mom quickly put on my performance make-up. I was already rattled due to getting up late, plus being nervous and add the freezing temperatures outside and I was shivering!

When we arrived at the concert I had to go immediately to the stage, it was my turn to dance! But as I started I began to forget my moves, the boy behind me was making me laugh. His eyes and ears looked funny. Plus he was dancing really slowly to a fast moving song. I just could not concentrate! Add to that my mom!

Every time I walked near my mother she said, "Baby! Look at the camera, Baby!" She was stalking me the entire day with a video camera! It was so embarrassing! All I could think was, Oh God, I want to hide! Even though I was busy and trying to ignore her, she kept repeating it over and over. All of the noise was making me crazy.

Finally, I screamed at the camera and started kissing my brother's faces everywhere. I know it was odd, but

I was really going crazy! At the end of the concert we all returned to the stage to sing along with the piano. I was singing and there was a different kid behind me singing so loudly that it hurt my ears! Why is it that there is always a crazy kid behind me and not someone else?! Seriously!

After the concert we went home. It had been such a busy day, and I was so tired that I felt like an old man walking with my hands in my pockets so slowly! Suddenly I felt the urge to run! Then I would walk slowly again. There I was running and walking randomly like some crazy person. Even though I was tired and feeling a little crazy, it was a special day for me.

Beautiful Sight

By Gaven Cary Collom

At the base of the mountains are the luscious green fields, laid out in the rooks and valleys between. Rocky and uneven at first, with many cracks and ruts spread throughout, they have jutting protrusions of unshapely stone cliff edges, but then gradually move into more fertile areas with trees and grass a dimmer and less vibrant than that of the greenery below, but a suitable alternative to the lifeless scraggly roots that cling to the rock base just below. And higher still from here the snow covered peak pierces into the air, a white contrast to the cloudless blue above, the most difficult treading of all. Spread out along the other side of the mountain and down onto the flat ground below is the brook, alive and thriving with fish of every kind. Beginning clear and clean, the water flows forcefully off a cliff near the bottom of the mountain, but calms into a slow but steady flow thereafter. Later along the stream the land turns boggy and swamp trees grow from the water and lilies and cattail line the edges. The trout and salmon of the clear part of the brook are gone; at this point among the green shaded water and gnats flying above are the bottom feeders, scavenging the muddy floor for algae and bacteria of sorts.

I made sure to take the sight in, for it was a beautiful one, and although there is no shortage of beautiful sights in this world, each needs to be remembered in its entirety to die to a well served life.

Colitis

By: Shianne Cross

When I was eight I was diagnosed with a disease called Colitis. It's something that makes your stomach hurt really badly. I told my mom (after a week of pain) and she made me a doctor appointment. When I went to the doctor I had my blood drawn and was told to come back the next day.

When I came back they told my mom that there was something wrong with me I was losing blood, was very dehydrated and I needed to go to the hospital to get fluids. I went to the hospital and was taken in for a scope. The scope took pictures inside my stomach and intestines. After the scope it was decided that surgery was necessary because my colin was swollen.

That was my very first surgery, I was nine years old. During the surgery I also had a port put in my chest. This is so medicine could be pumped easily into my body as I recovered. Awhile after surgery when every thing was looking good, the port taken it out. By that time a year had already passed and I was still doing badly. The doctor said that I had to have another surgery. This time to insert a tube into my arm.

When the surgery was happening, I missed out in half of 4th grade, Christmas, some of 5th grade and Halloween. I was really sick people sent me letters and my teachers brought my work to the hospital. My mom was always there for me. She stayed the night in the hospital with me and my dad came up there to visit when my mom had to work so that I had company and I wasn't always lonely. After the tube was put in my right arm the doctor said let's see how that goes for awhile. If it helps then it could come out later. By the time the surgery was complete I had to three blood transfusions because I had lost so much blood.

All together I had almost 15 blood transfusions. I was so scared because I was so sick, I thought I could have died. Thank god I have all my family members to support me and help me though everything. After my second surgery everything was kind of looking good until they took everything out. After awhile I had to be put on steroids because something wasn't going like they wanted it to. By that time I had gone to many different doctors to listen to what they thought was wrong. After all that was settled and I was taken off the steroids. I had to have another tube put in my left arm to get a different kind of medicine that I never had before. Things where looking good. I gained a lot of weight and my skin color wasn't so pale anymore. I was in school doing my work and I had a perfect appetite.

I had to go back to the hospital for a check up. The doctor said he wanted to give me a scope to look at my insides just to make sure everything was looking good. A few days passed and I went in for the scope. (When you have a scope you have to drink this liquid called Miramax it is really nasty. It's something you drink to clean your insides so that when they go inside your stomach they can see better.) When I went back for the scope I had a mask type thing on my face and had to breathe in this medicine that puts you right to sleep. I got to choose a flavor, I chose bubble gum. During a scope you are put under anesthetic while you're sleeping they import an IV so that you can get fluids.

I was finished with the scope about an hour later. The doctor told my mom that everything looked kind of good but there was still something they wanted to try. A month passed and then it was decided that I needed to get a colostomy bag. It's a procedure where they go inside your stomach and reattach things. While they were in the middle of doing that they took my appendix out too. After the surgery it was kind of hard for me to walk. I woke up with a tube in my nose so that I could breathe. My stomach hurt for so many days.

Eventually, I got to go home with my family, I was so excited. I was still in lots of pain but I was just so happy to finally lay in my own bed, take showers at my own house, eat my own food, smell fresh air and everything. When I got out everybody was excited to see me even though I looked really sick and I wasn't walking straight. I had the colostomy bag for about four months. I finally got it off in November. Three years had passed since all of these problems had started. I was so excited to have no more problems after that! I was able to participate in everything and anything. My mom was excited that I was able to walk not always lie down. I gained back my weight but still to this day I still have problems just not bad ones like before, I still am very skinny but I'm not very pale.

I think that overall I've been through a lot but I think I'm a strong person to have handled so much at such a young age. I have been through so much pain, been made fun of and I know what it's like to feel like you don't belong. But if there ever comes a day where something doesn't feel right it's always best to try to live through it because one day things will be right again.

October 25, 2010

By Daija Davis

I was sitting there, with nothing on my mind,
Counting the seconds; watching the time.
I regret it, not talking yet that day…
But little did I know, you weren't okay
No signs of you being gone, no time left.
I can't see you, anymore.
So now I'm sitting here, with way to much on my mind.
Counting the days, wondering how long it's been
And if you're wondering up there, I still regret it.
No, I'm not okay, wish you could've stayed.
I need you, I miss you, wish you never laid
Down, it's killing me slowly not seeing your smiles.
I don't know what it was, I done even know why, or when…
All I know is that you, were my
Best friend.
R.I.P. A.M.C.

Friendship

By Josselyn Diaz

You're my friend and that is true,
But the gift was given from me to you.
We went through moments that were good and bad,
Some that were happy and some were sad.

You supported me when I was in tears,
We stuck together through all our fears.
It's really sad that it had to be this way,
But it has reached its very last day.

Miles away can't keep us apart,
Because you'll always be here in my heart!
True friends are ones you can depend on,
Will always be there to defend you!

Friends share, friends care,
Friends know secrets other people don't know.
You can always count on them no matter what!
The good, the bad, the evil they've been through it too
We need friends everywhere!!

We Need a Phone

By Michael Dupuis

One day Brandon, Tyler and I were walking around. We needed a phone because Tyler needed to call his dad so we went to this car dealership called Tuff's. Tyler said, "Do you have a phone we can use?"

The dude said, "Did your car break down kid?"

Tyler said, "Forget it." We left, and the dude was staring at us. Tyler looked back. So we walked to a car dealership called GM. We said to this guy, "You got a phone?"

He said, "You leave your girls?" We started laughing and the dude said, "Yeah, I got a phone you need it?"

Tyler said, "Yes, please." We called our dads.

The dude said, "Why you need the phone?"

We said, "The guy at Tuff's was being mean to us."

The dude looked at me and said, "What's the story?"

I said, "I don't know ask Tyler."

The guy said, "Were you smoking?

I said, "No."

Tyler said, "The guy was staring at us when we left and he asked me if my car broke down and then he called me a kid. So we left and came here."

The GM guy said, "You know what you guys should do? We said, "What?"

He said, "You guys should go back there and egg his shop when it is closed."

I said, "Lets do it!"

Fireworks

By Grant Dzieciolowski

Every year we go,
To a very special place,
where I feel good.
The place with the shiny silver,
gold, red, white, and blue wrappers.

When we arrive there it is before me,
fireworks galore!
We walk in,
We are so excited,
All we can smell in this place is gunpowder
and explosive ingredients.

We scream loudly when we see those shiny colored
wrappers,
When those loud, crackly, things go in the air,
All the powder falls everywhere.

Down through the air,
Down into the trees,
Down then blown away by the breeze,
Fall burning chards of powder and paper,
and the sounds,
"Sssss" is the sound they make
when they reach the ground.

The 20th Annual Higgins Lake Trip

By Steven Else

It was the 20th annual camping trip. Our parents had started it 20 years ago and I have been there for the past six. So, this year it started off just like any other, except there were 15 people on a sinking boat in the middle of a lake.

Everything was getting taller… or was I getting shorter? Huh… What the… why were my feet wet? I looked down and the floor of the boat had a thin blanket of water over it. The water was going up, and so were the anxiety levels of the other fifteen people. Fifteen people to many apparently. The boat had finally stopped rocking from the huge ocean sized waves, but that was only because the boat was to low in the water to rock any more. Now was the time when people started pushing and jostling and before I knew it I was being thrown over board!

Oh no! The sea monsters got me! I feel it pulling me by my leg, this is the end, good bye cruel world! But wait! Once all hope seemed lost I burst through the surface one of the adults had my leg and was pulling me to the surface. I looked around and it became quickly apparent that we had no boat I look down and see the boat directly under me. I expected we were just going to leave it but my dad being the ol' cheapo refused to let that wretched boat sink! We all grabbed a side and slowly made our way back across the lake.

Abusing and Neglecting

By Alex Enriquez

What do you do when a dog is being neglected and abused? Dogs are hurt in many ways. Owners often adopt them just to give them away. Sometimes owners neglect them, but the police can come in to take them away. Neglecting dogs is a crime but people get away with it all the time.

Some owners treat their dogs like children. Others give them treats and teach them tricks, but sometimes they get sick of them. Who knows, dogs might be like a toy, you buy it and you throw it away when something else comes along.

I have family history with dogs being neglected or killed! My dads mom used to take my dads new born puppies, put them in a sack and hit them against the counter until the puppies died. After I heard about this, I barely talked to my grandma.

In the United States, almost 250 million cases of animal neglect and abuse are reported but only about 100 million cases are solved. Just think about how many dogs are dying each year - about 150 million dogs dying each year.

Hopefully, after reading my writing, you can how strongly I feel about dogs being neglected and abused. You can stop the abusing and neglecting by standing up and helping out at a dog shelter or just spreading the word around.

Stereos Pumping

By Tommy Fischer

Stereos pumping, studios banging.
All the pros are the ones I'm up staging.
Having my spirit and support is what I'm taking.
But don't look at my mistakes
Try and try how long can this take.
I shake the brace, hit the bass, rhyme flow go with grace.
Just look at my face.
I got pride in what I do.
It's not cheesy so no fondue.

I'm taking steps to the top and I'm counting them pacingly.
Taking minor falls but they only come occasionally.
I'm helping myself so you know I don't need catering.
As my name gets known these people keep on hating me.
I'm hyper so you know my rhymes always need a crazy beat.
And these influences are the one thing that is making me.
For all the people out there thanks for all the support.
And that opportunity you know I'm a go for it.
Cuz I buy everything so I ain't on a budget.
I got the rhythm bout partying cuz it-
Makes the mood better.
I'm the prime number one line go getter.
Get the party started, the paint I'm a go hard in.

The way you put flow is one of the things I'm twisting.
And the reason why I'm moving up is the thing you haters missing!

Stereos pumping, studios banging.
All the pros are the ones I'm up staging.
Having my spirit and support is what I'm taking.
But don't look at my mistakes
Try and try how long can this take.
I shake the brace, hit the bass, rhyme flow go with grace.
Just look at my face.
I got pride in what I do.
It's not cheesy so no fondue.

So fast I'm a move.
Kinda job you might need tools.
But I do it manually.
Mind wide open, just like a canopy.
My ratings go sky high, so outstandingly.
As I rise to the top other rappers vanishing.
It must be the way I'm handling.
Make a new mix tape yeah I will gladly.
Moving through all these haters is my favorite strategy.
I'm so intelligent so everybody mad at me.
So when I rise I'm a sit there happily.
Rhymes so good, flow feels like technically.
Skating all day so I move through them so I move steadily.
Flow complicated so some people ain't getting me.
And all the bills falling, they all trickling.

But no rain, so you still know my game, so you all know
I'm a keep it all the same.
And my head ain't clouded from all the fame.
If it ever does it'll be a shame.

Stereos pumping, studios banging.
All the pros are the ones I'm up staging.
Having my spirit and support is what I'm taking.
But don't look at my mistakes
Try and try how long can this take.
I shake the brace, hit the bass, rhyme flow go with grace.
Just look at my face.
I got pride in what I do.
It's not cheesy so no fondue.

Football

By Tyler Frase

Ever since I was 9 years old football has been my favorite sport. When we had our first practice we had to run so much and since it was my first year, I was out of shape from never doing it. I wanted to quit because it was so hard until, we had our first game. When we had our first game I realized that I actually liked football a lot and didn't want to quit! I really liked it. In football people always say that if you are bigger you are better. I don't believe that! When I was little I was bigger than most kids, and I had a small kid, half my size, hit me really hard! I couldn't believe it!

That year we went like six and two and made it to the second round playoffs, we lost to Clarkston. For my first year, my team was pretty good and we also had a lot of good athletes. The next year I ended up breaking my foot and was out the whole year! It was horrible!

My next year I was on varsity and we won every game! We even went to the super bowl and lost the super bowl to the Clarkston Chiefs. Since I was young the first year on varsity I got to play another year. That year we were really good too. We got a bunch of different players from everywhere, and we ended up winning every game. At the end of the season, we went down south to North Carolina for a tournament and we won all four games we played.

Football is my favorite sport. I just love the game and wearing the pads plus it is really fun to hit people with all your pads on and it's legal. Football has changed my life a lot. It teaches you how to stay in shape by working out. If you want to play high school football you should play football as young as possible so you can practice and learn how tackle right and everything. That's why football is my favorite sport and I will play it as long as I can.

Future Lost

By: Sabrina Gappy

The tragic event in September,
Many died while only few survived.
Going back, we may have seen this coming.
Maybe it could have been reversed,
We'll remember this forever.
Hearts were broken,
While the future was lost.
Memories were kept,
And family and friends were torn apart.
Wishing they could go back,
 And say their final words.
Tell them what'll be missed,
Hoping to see them soon.
Living everyday, hoping and waiting,
Taking precautions, and always praying.

A Dolphin Summer

By Kalee Garza

I got to swim with dolphins! How cool? If you ask me, it's one of the most awesome experiences of my life! A big whiplash splash sprung from the pool as the trainer blew her whistle signaling the dolphins to come to her. It's amazing how fast these beautiful animals can belt through the water.

As the dolphins swam I cautiously stepped into the cool, sparkly water. The trainer called for our group and we swam to meet her. As we approached, out of nowhere, came a huge SPLASH that happened, literally, two feet from me! The dolphin had swirled around and jumped, slapping his tail on the water, getting us in the face with his large wave! We all laughed, even the dolphin seems to laugh with us. The trainer lined us up so we could pet the dolphin. She spoke about the magical creatures and gave all kinds of facts about them. I was distracted by the amazing feel of their skin. Somewhat indescribable, the skin was dense, wet, smooth yet rough, rubbery yet buttery all at the same time. Imagine a spongy rock that has been weathered by the tide so that it becomes smooth and silky to the touch.

The trainer continued to take us through a series of interactions with our new friends from the sea. We took pictures, swam along side of them, and even learned actions to teach them during trick time. The trainer taught me a gesture and told me what to do, I had the dolphins waving their flippers at me and jumping and doing flips. It is truly astonishing what these animals are capable of doing. The dolphins received awards for their tricks and feeding them the gross smelly fish was my least favorite part. I think the dolphins thought getting their fishy rewards was the best part.

I have to say, as I reflect back on my trip to California last year, the highlight for me was the memories I have of my dolphin encounter. It was on my bucket list, I can now say I've done it! But more importantly, it is an amazing experience that many people don't get the chance to have. I feel lucky to have had a once in a lifetime experience, It was an incredible way to end a memorable trip.

Trapped

By Rebecca Gloden

It all happened so fast, one minute I was sitting on the beach listening to my Ipod, the next minute "he" snatched me from the pure white sand and threw me in some speed boat. The cold air was like a slap in the face as we sped away from the shore. The wind whistled through my hair, my cheeks had tears running down them that instantly dried in the fierce wind.

"What the heck is going on! Where are you taking me!" I screeched over the roar of the engine.

"Oh, you'll find out soon enough Calypso." The man said. He had thick black hair and tan skin. His accent was hard to place, but I was pretty sure it was Greek, maybe.

"How do you know my name!" I demanded.

"You escaped from your punishment, daughter of Atlas. So we must take you back to your island." He said, obviously.

"What!?! Are you insane! I'm not going to any island and my dad's name isn't Atlas it's Derrick!" I screamed.

"Oh spare me the innocent act, you can play that card all you want but I'm still taking you back to the wretched island."

I have to get out of here, I thought. Then I looked down at the dark blue water, and without a second thought I plunged in. It was colder than it seemed. The salt water stung my eyes, I came back up gasping for breath sputtering out water that was burning my throat. For one peaceful minute I treaded water and the blurriness in my eyes subsided. But it didn't last very long. I suddenly felt a sharp pain in my arm. I let out a agonizing groan and looked down, the water around me was a deep crimson and there right in my bicep was a steel dagger at least three inches deep. All I heard was the man's voice then I heard nothing, not even the steady gurgling of the speed boat. The colors went vivid then blurry, my legs felt like lead from treading, I was struggling to keep my head above water. I finally gave up then everything went black.

My eyes fluttered open when a strong hand grabbed my arm. My eyes fluttered open and the person in front of me was beautiful, but it was strange because this beautiful man had a white beard and usually people with white beards aren't that good looking. But he was, he had gray streaks going through his beard looking like lighting bolts, his eyes were a deep violet, and his skin had a deep tan with a white glow radiating from his body. I was out of breath when I saw his face.

He let out a mighty laugh when he saw that I was gasping for air.

"Poor little Calypso," he said , mockingly, "did you get lost in the ocean again?"

I started to raise a eyebrow then I noticed that the man and the boat were gone, then I looked down and the strange man and I were standing on the water.

"What the-how did you-what-what happened to the

man and the boat?" I said quickly, "how are we standing on water are you…a God?"

"Whoa there little Titaness take a breather, you know who I am."

I stared at him.

"Come on Calypso," he said "don't play stupid. Say it."

"Uhhhh… Santa?" I guessed.

"What? No!" He said angrily, "I'm the ruler of the Cosmos, the almighty Zeus!"

"Ummm ok… Zeus? I think that there's been a little bit of a mix up. I'm not the girl that everyone thinks I am. I am Calypso but not that Calypso," I explained. "I'm from Florida, I go to Colombia High School. So how about we just forget this whole thing ok? Just take me back to Florida and let's forget about this whole thing."

Zeus stared at me long and hard. Then he brought his face up closely to mine.

"Now listen to me Calypso," he put emphasis on the 'C' making spit go all over my face. "You have escaped your island more than once. We have been kind to you even though your father is a traitor to Olympus," Zeus said calmly. "So if you say one more thing about how the Gods are wrong about you, then so help me I will smite you with my lightning bolt so hard that you will blast into the deepest pits of Tartarus. Understand?"

I stared at him with my mouth gaped open. What did I do that angered these people so much? I asked myself. What island! I wanted to scream, but I didn't, I clamped my mouth shut. I turned away from the ruler of the Cosmos and said in a small voice.

"I understand."

When we finally arrived at the island I was appalled. Who would ever want to escape this island, it was gorgeous! The sand was pure white, the rocks were a silver metallic, beautiful gardens with: roses, lilies, tulips, and many more plants that I couldn't name. They all had the same silvery color. There were probably a million fireflies on the island. I was speechless.

It was the most beautiful place I've ever been to. The boat came to a gentle stop.

I stood so still that I gave Zeus a worried look, then I started to breathe again.

"It's so beautiful." I whispered, "why would anyone ever want to leave this island?"

"Probably because of the curse that comes along with it." Zeus said flatly.

"W-what curse?" I stuttered.

Suddenly the fireflies seemed to dim, the lively flowers now looked on the verge of death, and the silver rocks turned.

"The curse." Zeus said it like it was obvious. Then he sighed. "You must've hit your head really hard. I might as well start from the beginning. Many eons ago your father thought I was ruling the Cosmos wrong." Zeus explained through his teeth. "So he turned all the Gods against me, besides Aphrodite, because she was in the gardens, I was quick to act so before they could tie me up, I had Aphrodite flirt with your father. It was more effective than I would ever think." He chuckled. "My fellow Olympians snapped out of it and took my side. Atlas had to be punished. Then I thought of it. He would hold up the sky, what better punishment is there than to have a immortal Titan hold up the sky?"

asked Zeus, it wasn't really a question but he looked right at me.

"Uh, ok?"

"Ok? That's all you have to say." He said tightly.

"Fine! Yes, it's the best punishment I can think of." I said rolling my eyes. Zeus's eyes lightened and a smile spread across his face "I know it is!" Zeus beamed. The his expression turned stern "Never leave this island Calypso, Never."

Then he started to turn around.

"Wait." He stopped. "What's the curse?"

"Love. The cursc is love."

I knitted my eyebrows together. "Love? That's the curse?" I asked.

"Yes," Zeus nodded. "Many heroes will find this island but only once, that's it and when they arrive you will fall madly in love with each of them. They will love you too but won't be able to stay for some reason." Zeus smiled then…he was gone, just like that, I was alone and Zeus had taken the boat with him. I was stuck on the island with no way out.

I stood on the shore only hearing the crashing waves and crickets. Then without warning, I collapsed and started sobbing. I was trapped forever on this island for no reason, I wasn't the girl, and was confused about the God Zeus. A few hours passed by then out of no where I was blinded by a bright light. I looked up and standing there was Zeus and a girl that looked just like me.

"Who is this? I asked.

"This is the real Calypso, you liar!" Zeus said angrily.

"WHAT!" I screeched. "I never lied to you! This

whole time I've been trying to tell you this whole time I wasn't that girl but you never listened!" My voice went up three octaves.

"You never said any of that."

"Yes I did you idiot! I-"

"Silence!" He bellowed. "You have gone against the Gods one to many-"

"You're insane!" I screeched. "What's up with all this stuff about the Gods! Get a life!"

"That's it!" screamed Zeus. A lightning bolt appeared in his hands. " You had your warning now your going to pay the price!"

He lifted the lightning bolt over his head then hurled it straight at me.

"No!" I shrieked.

I bolted up right in my bed. Lightning flashed through my window making me jump.

"It was just a dream?" I looked around. "It was just a dream!" I started cracking up. I couldn't stop. Then I heard a knock at the door, the person who knocked came in.

"Is everything okay in here? He asked.

When I saw the person I started screaming. I couldn't believe who it was. When I stopped screaming I was able to choke out the name.

"Zeus!" A smile spread across his lips.

A Friend

By: Destiny Goldsmith

A friend is someone special,
Very close to your heart,
To laugh right beside you,

Every day from the start.

A person you have silly handshakes with,
Even if they are very dumb,
and even if they make both your hands numb.

A friend is someone who knows all your secrets,
A person you can trust,
and will always have your back
and that's a big must.

A friend is someone you can talk to,
For at least and hour long,
someone who will stick be you even if you're
wrong.

Someone who gives you the best advice,
No matter what you ask,
the advice they give you should
always fulfill the task.

A person you do facial masks with every Saturday
night,
And will always save a spot for you
even when it's tight.

A friend is someone you go to the mall with,
And have lots of fun,
and don't care how many bags you have
even though there's a ton.

A friend is someone who is true to you,
Even though its rough,
someone who always sticks by you even when its
tough.

A person you go to the movies with,
Even if you see someone you don't like,
and bite your tongue so you don't tell them to
go and take a hike.

Xbox

By Angelo Gonzales

Xbox is a very fun entertainment system. It has many games you can play and hundreds of demos you can download. Xbox is made by Microsoft which is an American made company. It is run by Bill Gates, who is a very famous business man and the richest in America. Microsoft is always compared to Sony which is a Japanese company that makes similar electronics to Microsoft. They are famous for making the world famous Play Station. This is another gaming system similar to Microsoft's Xbox.

Most people sat Xbox is better, but different people have different opinions. Most people that play Xbox go on Xbox Live. Xbox Live is an online network where you can play anyone that has an Xbox around the world. You can also talk to them like you're on the phone and text them while playing the game. It is one of the most enjoyable features if not the best feature about the system. There is always someone online playing the game you are playing because it is so popular. You can make your own character and make it look like you for the word to see.

Summer Sun

By: Emilie Guanzon

As day ends
Night gradually begins…
In quiet serenity I take in the beautiful view.
The light blue sky turns a fiery crimson;
Bold pinks, yellows, oranges, and reds gradate the sky.
White cotton candy clouds fade to light gray as the wind blows.
The sun's magnificent beams glisten onto the deep, blue ocean.
Powerful waves quietly recede from shore,
Leaving seashells, seaweed, and pebbles behind.
A slight breeze triggers palm leaves to brush against each other.
Slowly, the sun shrinks behind the horizon.
As it fades to a blur,
The moon peaks out while the stars twinkle…
Deliberately, everything changes.
The sky blackens,
And the ocean blends within,
Waves continue, sand dissipates,
Night has finally come.

Crying Pain

By Ronisha Hall

I sit there crying in pain because
Someone I love is gone.
Saying to myself,
How could this happen?

There she is laying there,
In a coffin.
Peacefully,
Leaving me.

Tears drizzle down my face,
I can barely breathe.
Stomach hurts, head aches.
Feel like I might faint.

Saying good bye is so hard!
More tears roll down my face.
Somehow I wish she'd come back,
Someday, somehow.

I had to let my grandma go.
I have to continue,
And achieve my dreams.
That's what she'd want me to do.

The funeral's over.
Days go past.
I still cry the pain away,
Every night and every day.

I learned to let go of the past
And to start all over again.

Two Poems

By Cameron Halls

Sad
Head hanging low
A frown on his face
Head looking down
A tear in his eye
Like a lost puppy
So frightened and scared
Just feeling so blue
Alone and afraid
No smiling or laughing
Just frowning and crying

Inspired
A smile on your face
Chin up high
Walking with a strut
Butterflies in your gut
Like a soaring eagle
Proud with Opportunity
Inspired the greatest emotion of all
A great feeling
After a huge downfall

Imagination Poems

By Brendan Hanson

Imagining and pondering are as different as can be,
Pondering can be stressing and very anxious
 It is dumb worries dumped on the mind
With obnoxious consideration around the corner
And not fun at all,
With no happy memory to spare.
Imagining can be different
You can create a luscious forest with tons of life
Or a fantasy stories never told
Maybe a fantasy story from the old
It's like the season spring with the sprout of stories
Wondrous adventures and perils through imagination
It is more than just thoughts, it's a wondrous story

Dream
Ideal, vision
Imagining, trancing, fantasizing
Children, teachers, teachers, strategists
Thinking, reflecting, reasoning
Deliberate, mediate
Ponder

Homerun

By Cody Happ Neiger

One game during baseball season. It was a few weeks after I broke my hand at a friend's house. I didn't know it was broken and I made a good decision to go to my baseball game. I'm glad I went my hand still hurt but I didn't think much of it after all it was the second to last game of the season and I just couldn't miss it. After I tried playing in the field with my acing hand it was time for my team to bat. All of my teammates that batted made it on base.

Then it was my turn to bat. I was so worried about my broken hand I couldn't even speak I had know choice as I stepped up to the plate I got ready to swing. The ball came I swung and bam. All I saw was the ball rocketing through the field. I didn't have much time to gloat I had to run like the wind and I did. I was already at first base and they hadn't even had the ball yet. I passed first and was worried about second base and they had the ball. I passed second and was almost to third and then. I saw the ball flying in the air from the outfielder. This was my time to shine. I passed third and rocketed towards home. They threw the ball to the catcher I ran I slid and I barely missed the tag by an inch.

After I passed home plate the crowed started cheering it made me feel so good plus and this was my only homerun in history. When I went back to the bench

I just realized the pain in my hand. It was a horrible pain but I was tuff and didn't show it and the game went on as normal. A few weeks later my hand was still hurting I told my parents they took me to the doctors. After the x-rays they came back and told me it was broken and that I couldn't play baseball for a few weeks. I was crushed because I couldn't play my last championship baseball game. Even though I had to where a cast I still went to my last game to support my team. Also I was bummed out because I couldn't do anything and I couldn't play my last baseball game. Ill never forget that homerun and that hand injury. My hand is better now and IV started playing baseball again. I'm still trying to get more homeruns but I don't think ill get another one like when I broke my hand. A lot of people say my broken hand was my good luck charm. But I say it was my team that helped me through it all!

Poem

By Brian Heath

Bored
Sitting there words blazing,
The haze not phasing,
Outside steady gazing stars shinning,
Thinking about the world behind me,
My life so nice,
His so mean,
Could have been a dream,
Hallucinating seeing things,
People thinking where's his brain,
Not talking about those fruits and grains,
I'm highly trained,
Can't stop getting this stuff,
Going home every day keep getting it ruff,
Thinking about the other guy,
Why do you think of this stuff,
But think were you ever good enough,

Happy Being Me

By Haley Helchowski

With no hesitation I grab it from the rack, but with a lump in my stomach I put the size 2 little black dress back. I couldn't stand the fact of my dad writing a hundred dollar check. I start to question if fashion is my passion, if modeling is my thing. There's not many of me, no I don't call my self a skinny wannabe. I want to be myself and no one else. I want to be the girl who loves to cheer and swim. The girl who thinks, that everyone should win. The girl would rather give then get. I'm not a size two, three or four. I'm a size ten plus a couple more. I love singing and cooking and sometimes I'll be bad and steal a cookie while none is looking. I can't stand the thought of spiders or snakes just the sight of them makes my heart race. I love my family and friends the laughter never ends. I always have a smile on my face. Though I'm not perfect and my things are always out of place. I always try my best and do whatever it takes. I have no problem taking second place. My hair never looks great. My clothes must be pristine and fit for a queen. They call me crazy I saw in love because everyday it feels like I'm

F
L
O
A

T
I
N
G
Above

Looking down on my world the place I call home, Feeling sorry for those who are alone. I want to be their friend because that is who I am. I am a classic. I don't have to be size two or twenty three. I am perfectly happy being authentic. Happy being me!

Life or death

By Josie Lynn Hempton

As I sit in this room
    I start to think that I am doomed.
        I start to feel cold
           I wonder if I will ever grow old.
I start to cry
    I wonder if I am going to die.
        The door opens and I see light.
        I knew that I will live tonight.
I get out of this nightmare
    Until I find that it is good night
        He hit me with a shovel and knocked me
        out cold.
        Then I knew that tonight I would never
        grow old

That Unexpected Night

By Lucas Hendricks

Four boys out for a night of fun,
They would never expect to call 9-1-1.
Messing around making bad decisions,
The night of their life was their vision.
One huge mistake getting into the car,
It seemed to be going very well so far.
Then the driver's vision started to blur,
The passengers did not know where they were.
The driver losses control and the car quickly spins,
The panicking and screaming starts to begin.
Another driver heading home at night,
Couldn't see the other car due to the bright lights.
A crash and a spin once the cars collide,
Sadly the innocent driver has died.
The drunken teen climbs out of the wreck,
He hopes his friends are alive but doesn't check.
Now the only survivor the one people blame,
Sits in a jail cell living the future in shame.

Soccer

By: Ivan Hernandez

In the locker room.
The stadium under the moon.
They lace up they're cleats.
They walk out, hoping not to get beat.

They're out on the field, hear the crowd cheer.
Then the crowed shushes nothing to hear.
They walk in order, step in line.
You listen to that song that shows country pride.

The crowd starts again screaming and cheering.
Some fans out there crying and tearing.
They step in the middle, time to flip the coin.
The rest go in to see and join.

They get this feeling straight in your heart.
Just to see the home team gets to start
They're in the middle of the field ready to go.
Waiting for the sound of the whistle to blow.

They kick the ball, the clock starts to run.
They pass to the left and pass to the right and already
you think "wow that looks fun".
He's down the middle, his teammate to the left
Then you notice he's all set

He passes the all through the defensive wall.
Then you notice he has the ball.
He sees the opportunity, again that feeling back in
They're heart.
He takes the shot; then you say 'what an early start".

The crowd jumping, kicking so happy and glad.
The guys next to them are all angry but sad.
You look at the replay "that's a nice kick"
Then you say "what a nice back flip"

Nothing else happens the rest of the time.
But you still watch the field as green as a lime.
Suddenly, you see the visitors with an amazing trick.
But, what a save by the goal keeper but, it's a corner kick.

They get the ball, it was tossed
Then you see such a great cross.
A man jumps for the header, as little as a troll.
The announcer says "what a great goal".

That goal was a paralyzer.
Unfortunately there's the equalizer.
But, the referee had to ruin all the fun.
The whistle blows, the first half is done.

The teams come out again for the next meet.
Some fans still coming back to their seats.
The teams still wait for the whistle to call.
This time it's the other team's ball.

90 minuets almost pass, some fans smiling, some grinning.
You take a look at the score, no one is winning.
You notice they got the steal.
You see the away team moving up field.

They pass to the right they pass to the left
The spin move, left the goal keeper for dead.
No one there to block the strike.
He hits the ball with almost no might

The announcer says "they made the break through"
Look at the defender and you know that he knew.
You look at the time its probably lost.
You think these tickets weren't worth the cost.

You look up and see, they're making a run, very quick.
He gets stop with a hit.
Horrible challenge, not a pretty hit.
Fortunately it's a penalty kick.

Last chance to make one more.
If not then our team is done for.
He sets up the ball ready to kick.
Hoping the goal keeper won't make a hit.

Fans on they're feet to see the result.
Hoping the penalty won't be a fault.
The referee sounds ready to go.
When all of a sudden "ohhh what a great goal!"

Everyone leaves not happy or sad.
The away fans leave, fairly mad.
Nobody won and nobody lost.
To think this all happened with one coin toss

The Panther

By Thomas Hilborn

Terry quickly grabbed his tent, pistol, and a hunting knife. He then started hiking toward the mountain where a panther named Cerebral had been killing off most of the big game.

After hiking for three hours, Terry finally found a small clearing of trees on the mountain, Terry started setting up his tent. Putting his pistol on a nearby log, he began to snap twigs and sticks to make a clearing on the forest floor.

Pausing to wipe some sweat off his brow, he heard a low guttural growl coming from behind him. His hunter instincts kicking in, he snatched his gun from the log and shot in the direction the growl originated. Spinning around, he saw the panther Cerebral charging at him and the shot had missed. Seeing that Cerebral was now ready and tensed to pounce, Terry put all his weight on his left leg and jumped sideways out of the way.

Quickly regaining his balance, Terry aimed his pistol at Cerebral's head. Grinning, Terry closed his finger around the trigger and pulled. But nothing happened. The gun had jammed.

His grin faded, Terry tossed away the pistol and reached down to his leg holder and pulled out his hunting knife. Renewed with determination, Cerebral charged at him and Terry started slashing madly with his knife. This only managed to make a slight cut across Cerebral's face.

Being knocked down by the force of a panther, Terry's grip on the knife loosened. Seeing her chance, Cerebral batted the knife out of Terry's hand.

Struggling in a futile effort to get Cerebral off, he saw the opening mouth of the panther. It quickly went toward his neck. Then his vision went black and he knew nothing.

Moving

By Robby Holderread

On May 5th I will be moving into a new house. I won't be going to a new school or anything but its kind of weird thinking about living in a new house. I've lived in my house for almost eleven years now and I'll only be in our new one for about four years. Even though moving doesn't bother me, it's still weird thinking about living in a new house.

After living in this house for this long of you get a lot of memories and stuff. In the new house we won't have any memories of any good times to be reminded of; we will get to make new ones. I think I will feel weird living in a new house because it will be like living in someone else's house. You now when your afraid to touch stuff because you might break it.

I'm also excited to move because the new house will be better and bigger. The new house has a smaller yard so there's not as much to clean up in the fall. There's also a shed where we can keep stuff instead of in the garage. That way there will be room in the garage for the cars.

Since we only have one truck and five people to help, it will take a long time to move. We didn't want to spend the money on a moving truck when we didn't have to. A big problem will be getting the furniture out the doors since it barely fit going in. We might get some help from some other people though which would help out a lot.

We have a lot of work to do to our old house before we can start to move into our new one. We have to do a lot of painting, remove our old rugs, and then we have to clean out from under the rugs that have been there for about ten years. We also have to take our furniture to our new house. The hardest thing we'll have to move will be our 64" T.V. that we'll have to take completely apart and put back together, and hope we don't break it. I hope that this house will make a great home.

Wounded Knee

By Alex Hollis

My heart was pounding, chest throbbing, adrenalin rushing terror through my body as I made my way across this dangling bridge. The bridge was stretched between two giant mountains swaying dangerously miles above the ground. I was thinking to myself, "How high is this bridge?" I really didn't want to know because about twenty feet below the bridge all you could see was fog. I was carefully making my way across the bridge. I had made it to the middle of the bridge when a huge gust of wind rocked it back and forth. I was desperately trying to keep my footing, but my sister was behind me and she grabbed my leg to keep from falling. Between the wind and my sister I didn't last long, I tripped and fell hard onto my knees. As I stood I could see that my knees were bleeding badly.

My brother came running to help us make it off the bridge and then carefully to our truck. When he got me to the truck I sat on the tailgate, my mom brought me a towel and some gauze to wrap around my knees. They didn't want me getting into the truck until the bleeding slowed or stopped. So I sat with the towel while my mom went shopping. She returned to the car with a pair of sunglasses for me and a necklace. She told me to get in the car so we could leave and head back to the cabin we were staying in.

The next morning when everyone was getting up and getting ready to leave I opened the door and started down the stairs. Suddenly, SMASH! I tripped and fell on my knees! The bleeding started all over again!

My Story

By Emily Howard

You hurt me, and broke me.
I gave you every ounce of me.
You could never say that I didn't try , or that I gave up.
I did everything I could and it just wasn't good
enough for you.
You never saw the girl behind the mask.
You will never know who I am , or saw the real me
You could not possibly know the damage you have
caused.
I see you with your friends.
You act like nothing ever happened.
I'm not afraid of what people think of me.
But I can clearly see you are.
I can be the real me and not be ashamed.
I'm goofy , weird , kind , and fun.
I'm ok with all of that
But I'm not sure you are.
The fun in being in a relationship is that you can be
your self.
Not be scared that they will not like the real you

A Bottle's Voice

By FangTing Huang

UGH...UGHH!.. UGHHHH!!! I am so so board, this is so boring, I hate this place its dark and it's too cold. GET ME OUT OF HERE ALREADY!!!!!!!!!!

Beep-Beep-Beep, someone's coming!! , please get me out of this boring, dark, and cold place, clank-thump-clank-hiss.

Ugh not again, when is it going to be my turn to get out and see the world, feel the sunshine on my body as the person puts me down on a table, feel the wind as it cools me down while the person rides a bike.

Clank-clank-clank-clank-clank-clank-clank-clank-clank. Bye everybody I know, everybody I knew my whole life.

Clank (change goes in)-beep-beep-beep-beep-beep-beep (button's pushing against the machine) - rattle-rattle-rattle-rattle (bottle going down the whole machine) - thump (bottle in the little hole) - than a hissss (the cap of the water bottle is being twist open).

I AM FREE, finally free of this horrible place. Now I can feel the sunshine, see the world, feel the wind.

YAHOO!!!! Wow it is so hot outside and I am sweating a lot but I am not going to whine or complain about it because this is what I have been waiting for my whole life.

After 1 hour, I am sooo HOT!!! I need to find a place where theirs shad or someplace else that is cool.

LACROSSE FIGHT!

By Brandon Jardon

So it was four o clock and I was doing home work and then had to get ready for my lacrosse game that I had against Royal Oak. They were an ok team but our team was better our team name is the Waterford Falcons we had only lost 1 game and they already lost 3.

I was ready for this game but the Royal Oak team we vs. last year was talking a lot of carp and acting all tough towards us. So I 3was thinking if it was going to be the same team or if it was a different team. I knew it was the same team when we got there because they were talking crap to us already. And the game hasn't even started yet this was going to be fun.

So first quarter of the game we scored once we had one penalty and they had 4. They were stalling the ball a lot in the 2nt quarter and playing a good defense so we didn't score that round.

And the score was 1 to nothing now it was the 3rd quarter and we were going out with our best defense and we scored 2 times at the end of the 3rd quarter I here the other coach say go hard and hit a lot. So it was 4th quarter and they were laying our guys out left and right but also they were getting a lot of penalties. Then at the face off the Royal Oak kid pushed one of our kids to the ground and started punching for no reason.

So one of our team mates stepped in to help our

team and the 2 more Royal Oak kids jumped in and it was 2 on 3. So then another one of our guys jumped in and then they were fighting like crazy until a ref broke it up. 3 of our guys got kicked out for the game and only one of there's did. There was five minutes left in the 4th quarter. And we scored twice and were playing a good defense and won the game 5 to zip.

Daffodils

By: Shubham KC

It's noon dear daffodils; it's time to go,
I don't want to leave you but I need to go,
Let's go daffodils to church to pray
We'll be friends forever you say!

It's dusk now; its time to go,
I don't want to leave you, but I need to go,

It's a night; its time to go
I never want to leave you but I need to go
It's a late; go to bed
Oh dear daffodils I miss you yet.

It's morning there's a pearl of dew,
Oh dear daffodils I miss you too!

Love and Hate

By: Kyle Kennedy

I get up out of bed,
got this stupid game in my head.
Dream at night of taking flight,
just soaring, roaring,
eventually destroying.
My team goes up, but I'm benched.
Feel like a wrench.
Yeah a tool! A complete fool.
Feel like I am being used,
to give my team a break,
just because I might make a mistake.
The buzzer goes off,
and I'm finally in!
Going for the win - but I just get faked out,
the coach is thinking about taking me out!
No, wait! I get the ball,
Not letting my team fall-
I take the shot,
but I fell like a robot,
programmed to miss.
I wish I could be as good as the rest of the team,
but maybe that'll just always be a dream.
I get out of bed,
with this stupid game in my head.
Dreaming of just taking flight,

just soaring, roaring,
ultimately destroying .
Now my hand's shaken.
My world's quaking.
I think I might be mistaken.
The butterflies in my stomach,
I think a might plummet,
right back down to realty,
where I suck at everything!
This team just might be a match for me.
But never know just wait and see.
You ain't taking this game away form me.
I'll be back next quarter,
Showin' you why it's better being taller,
Rather than shorter.
I get up out of bed,
and got this stupid game in my head.
I dream at night of taking flight,
and just soaring, roaring,
just destroying.

We were down by four,
when I hit the floor,
I was ready to send them OUT THAT DOOR!
Cuz' I got skill you can't ignore,
and I'm about to grab that ball and go hardcore!
Yeah, soarin' now cuz I'm way better than before.
Dats right you know I just scored!
now hold up,
there's two more,
now slow up,

we just need to hold that score,
now post up,
we can't let them rush that board
we've got a minute to win-it,
and our defense is rocking,
yeah you know we're knocking!
them way down to size,
cause the clock just ran out,
and they finally met their demise.
I get up out of bed,
and got this stupid game in my head.
I dream of night of taking flight,
and just soaring, roaring,
just destroying.

Choices

By Katelyn Killewald

Deep deep down in my heart
I feel like something is pulling,
My heart is telling me one thing,

My head is telling me something different.
If I choose one I will lose the other,
I search and search, and I'm trying to find the solution
I'm looking for,
But I can't get my hands on the answer.

To some people it's and easy choice,
To me it may take a life time to decide.
Which is more important?
Which path should I choose?
It's up to me decisions, decisions.

Shopping

By Yeirim Kim

I shop non-stop,
Even when I need to take a pit stop.
On my twelfth shop I start to drop,
But then I see a cute top!

As I browse with excitement my eyes dart,
To an outfit from far away.
I run to the rack of clothes fast,
Pushing people that pass.

As all the attention was 0n me,
It built my tension and anxiety.
Reaching closer to the shirt,
My legs start to hurt.

I am on red alert,
But it didn't stop me.
I grabbed the top
Feeling ready to jump a lot!

Squealing with joy,
but trying to be coy,
the entire store I did annoy!
I know I still want more…

Off we go to another store.

LIFE WARNING

By Marinna Kinaya

Best Friends-WARNING:

May make you laugh so hard you cry. Makes you remember inside jokes and old memories. If it is swallowed you might throw up secrets. You could encounter with the following: gossip, rumors, happiness, and smiling. Thinking the same thing as each other may occur. Avoid talking behind your friends back and don't tell on them. If you do one of these deadly things your friendship can end quickly and dramatically

Family-WARNING:

You may fight with family members. You could find random cuts, bruises and scratches all over your body; and do not know how it came upon you. You could suffer from embarrassment. It is possible that you can be exposed to mini-van mom syndrome. These symptoms can include: loving, controlling, strict, over-bearing, nosey, and annoying parents. It is not recommended to answer back, have attitudes, not clean room, or not do your daily chores. If you do you can get grounded from you're: phone, computer, television and ipod.

RISKS:

Having these people in your life could be very life threatening and dangerous. If you over dose that means: you can die, you may be crazy or mentally ill, and you could end up in a hospital or rehab. Use at your own risk.

Florida

By: Bri Kouzoujian

It was 103 degrees outside in Orlando, Florida...far too hot to walk around any of theme parks in Walt Disney World. My mom and I decided to go to one of the water parks; it was called Blizzard Beach. As soon as you stepped into the park you saw a very steep water slide going straight down. 152 feet in the air, with just one steep drop, but why was there a ramp going off half way down the slide? When I went on it I figured out that just before the ramp is a hole so they make you think you're going to fly off the ramp, but really, you're going down a hole.

My mom and I were standing in line for a raft ride when a stranger with very dark brown and blue eyes said to us in a deep British accent, "Do you just fly off that water slide?!" He was pointing toward the ride I'd just gone on with the steep drop. At first I was a little confused, is this guy serious? Why would they make a water slide were you fly off at 100 feet in the air? The guy looked like he just saw a ghost; I could tell he was freaked out by the water slide. That's when I realized he wasn't kidding and he was completely serious. "Umm no, you don't fly off; there is a little hole right before the ramp that you go down. The guy let out a deep breath; he looked very relieved, "Okay! Thank you so much!" He said and walked off.

As soon as he was out of our sight my mom and I lost it. We were laughing historically; tears were coming out of our eyes. We couldn't believe some idiot actually though Walt Disney World would make a water slide that you fly off of and die. We were amazed at ourselves that we didn't start laughing when he asked us that question. This happened about three years ago and even now when we talk about Florida, this memory always comes up and we still act like it is the funniest thing on Earth.

Escape

By Samantha Krapohl

The poor girl. She never seems to get enough sleep. I guess that's what happens when you infuse someone's blood with mercury.

Technically, there's some bromine and silicon powder in the mixture as well, but that's beside the point. The important part is what it can do – and it was life changing. Literally. The children infused with the solution – before birth, of course – could do amazing things. Surreal, unbelievable things.

She stirred; her inhuman senses must have noticed my presence. Her eyes opened, and seeing me, she shot up – almost hitting her head on the top of her cage. I eyed it, looking up and down. Those things were far too small. It was three feet on each side, and four and a half feet tall – my intern training had told me that – but it looked so much smaller.

"Well?" Kate practically yelled. She truly hates me. I'd call it hormones, but she had a reason to hate me. I worked for the people that did this to her.

"I just came to bring news. Your father..." Her expression of pure disgust stopped me up short. She hated him more than she hated me. He had injected the solution personally.

"Your father is taking you away with him," The brightness in her eyes killed me. "For a test." I watched her happiness vanish – she'd thought she was going to be free. I sighed inwardly; she would never be free. The only escape from this horrid place was death.

I shuddered. I had to keep thoughts like that out of my mind.

"What kind of test?" she asked, wariness and anger seeping through her voice. She grabbed the bars of her cage, and I saw them start to shake. Uh-oh.

I know Kate, I've known her for years, so I know when she's about to break. Working in this lab for eighteen years lets me know what happens when a subject like Kate breaks.

I jerked open the door to her cage as quickly as I could, and she leapt out, sending it flying across the room. Wow, was she strong.

"Calm down, Kate, just calm down…" I put a hand on her shoulder, but she ripped it off. There was no way I could get her to relax. I backed away, stopping when I reached the medical tray behind me. I felt around, hands behind my back, and found the hypodermic needle I was looking for. It was filled with an improved version of morphine that looked and smelled like normal saline, but was actually a strong anesthetic. I flicked off the cap and got ready to jab it into her arm.

"Answer me!" she yelled. "Now!"

What she wanted was classified information. What she wanted could get me fired. What she wanted was the one thing I couldn't tell her. But I had to…it was the only thing I could do for her.

Or was it?

I hid the needle up sleeve and put my hands up, feigning defeat. I slowly approached her, trying to convey my message. I wasn't going to hurt her. I was going to help her.

"Kate, you have to understand...one day, it'll all make sense." I plunged the needle into her arm, only allowing about a fourth of it to make it into her bloodstream. I only needed her out for about an hour. By then, she'd be smuggled onto a plane headed for some far-off, uncharted island.

She stared up at me, hatred and confusion hidden behind the fog in her eyes. She'd be asleep in less than a minute, and both of us knew it. "Why?" she whispered. 'Why' was a good question. I knew what I was going to do, and I knew I had to do it, but why? Would life in some distant jungle be better than a life in this terrible lab? My immediate answer would be yes, and I'm sure hers would be too, but was it right? In the long run, would she be safer here?

"Why?" she whispered once again. I saw the awareness slipping out of her face, and I knew I only had seconds left to talk to her. That's when I decided.

"I'm going to get you out of here, Kate," I said. Her eyes slid closed, and I lifted her up off of the ground. As I stared at her sleeping face, I made myself a promise. Kate will be free, if it's the last thing I do.

Inspiration

by Samantha Krapohl

True inspiration doesn't fall into your lap –
You have to look for it in the world around you.
In the sway of the grass,
The shimmer of the sun,
The glint in the pond.
In the chirp of a bird,
The creak of a tree,
The whisper in the wind.
If you open your eyes
To the beauty of the world,
You'll find what you've been looking for.
Open your arms
For inspiration to come
And it will.
Trust me.

The Storm

By Austin Lazenby

A calm cool day,
The sky is clear,
"The day is bright."
A mother said.

A cloud rolled in,
Gray as the night sky.
"A storm is brewing."
The old man whispered.

The rain began to fall,
So hard it pelted the townsfolk.
"A storm is coming!"
The man's wife yelled.

The bells struck through the air,
Like a scream at a horror house.
The winds picked up,
Leaves were flying.

The winds calmed down,
The sky turned murky green.
"A storm is here!"
A child screamed.

A funnel came down,
Trees were uprooted,
Buildings torn apart,
The church bell cut off.

All was silent.
The clouds swept away.
The storm was over,
But the village was gone.

Missing You

By Madeline Long

Don't stand there and pretend like you know what I'm
going through;
you don't know anything.
Don't ask me if I'm okay when I'm crying;
I'm not okay.
Don't get offended if I'm not talking to you;
I'm in a bad mood.
Don't call me a liar when I tell you what happened;
I wouldn't lie about that.
The saying "You don't know what you have until it's
gone" is true.
I regret the phone calls I didn't answer and the visits I
skipped.
She's gone.
I miss my mom.

October 14, 1959 ~ April 7, 2011

My Troubles, My Pain, My Everything

By: Haley Lönnemo

Day by day time goes by.
I think about you
your always on my mind.
I feel the pain as time passes by.

I wish you were here right by my side.
It's been days, it's been months
when will this pain ever stop?

Today was a nightmare.
And so was yesterday;
I wish it would all just fade away.

I hide the sting of you passing away.
I'm so sorry you had to go that way.
You were my life, you made my days.

You got me through all those tough things:
My troubles, my pain, my everything.
People always say the ache goes away.
Maybe in a few years, or even days.

But is this even true?

Because everything reminds me of you.
All the pain comes back to heart,
when I see that picture of you.

This is how I would feel
if you were to go away.
But I thank God everyday
for him letting you stay.

I love you mom
please don't ever go away.
Till death do we part?
We've been together from the start.

Out of Control

By Maranda Lossia

The impact of the car
Made the glass shatter.
When the police came
They made the crowd scatter.

The ambulance came,
They took her away.
I sat wondering
If she would be okay.

I walked through the hospital,
With sleep winning a fight.
It was hard to remember
What happened that night.

The light turned green
And we ended in a crash.
Now our shiny car
Was a piece of trash.

After a few hours
The doctor said,
Without a doubt,
She is dead.

I said to myself
Nothing can tear us apart.
With great memories we had,
She will always be in my heart.

Parrots

By Rafael Maldonado

Parrots can be very good pets. They are very intelligent animals. Parrots come from may different parts of t he world from South America to Africa these little, well not all of them are little, birds love to chew on plants, paper, and just about everything else.

The size of a parrot usually varies between species. They could be a small Love Bird which is one of the smallest types of parrots usually about 5 to 7 inches long, weighing between 40 to 60 grams to a gigantic Macaw which can be between 12 to 40 inches long and weigh between 4.5 oz to about 3.75 Ib and can sometimes talk!

Parrots can be very good pets, like the love bird for instance it's a small very affectionate parrot, but usually cannot speak (in a human language). Parrots will usually require a lot of attention from there owner if they don't have a mate, and are sometimes know to chirp or squawk very loudly in the morning and at night or when they want attention.

Parrots in the wild generally eat seeds, nuts, fruit, buds and other plant material. The most important food in most true parrots diets are seeds which would explain why most parrots have a large and powerful bill capable of cracking open some of the toughest of seeds.

Some large parrot species, including large cockatoos,

amazons, and macaws, have a very long lifespan, with 80 years being reported and record ages of over one hundred. Small parrots, such as Love Birds, Hanging Parrots, and Budgies have shorter life spans of up to about15–20 years. As pets there are some problems with such long life spans some larger parrots outlive there owners.

The intelligence of parrots is absolutely astounding, parrots can a lot of times mimic human voices but some Gray African Parrots have been known to be able to be able to associate words with their meanings and form simple sentences. Not only have parrots demonstrated intelligence through scientific testing of their language-using ability, but some species of parrot such as the Kea are also highly skilled at using tools and solving puzzles.

Mimo

By: Nicole Manga

I remember when I first got you
Little as can be,
You looked up
and I knew we were meant to be.
I picked you up and held you
Knowing for sure that you and I
Would have the best memories.

The cat I'd always wanted,
Now would be called Mimo!
I knew that name would fit you!

When I saw that you had
more toes then a cat really needs.
I knew this made you different
But very special to me!

I loved how you had black and white
All over your body
These colors made you special
And unique as can be.

I remember
You playing catch,
And trying to climb trees-
Never stopping to rest, or even eat.

Or that day you ran away,
When I was shocked and dismayed.
I thought I would never find you.
So I looked for you all day,
Until I finally grabbed you
And made you stay.

After our very long days
It was time to sleep
You would follow me to bed,
And purr deeply.

Mimo, I hope you know
I loved you very much.
If I ever get another pet,
They will never be
As special as you were to me.

You were only three
Why did you have to leave?
Now who will I go to
When I feel lonely?

You were in so much pain
I knew, but did not want to believe
Very soon I'd have to let you go
And say bye to my little kitty.

Basketball

By Jacob Midkiff

Basketball is a fast game,
It is not at all lame.
You get to shoot an orange and black ball,
The M.V.P's are very tall.

The game is played with a hoop,
An exciting move is an alley-oop.
Another play is the full court press,
That play really makes a mess.

You get baskets if you are fast,
But if a player breaks his nose,
He has to wear a mask.
The jump ball signals the stat of the game.

Let's Stand Tall

By Sarah Murphy

You walk into school, it's Monday and the whole school is practically asleep on their feet. You, on the other hand, are excited to show off the new outfit you got over the weekend! You head for your locker, head held high, when you feel eye's on you. You turn your head to look around. That's funny, you could've sworn those girls in the corner were looking at you. Oh well, you're probably just seeing things. You arrive at your locker when, suddenly those girls who'd been in the corner walk by, giggling and pointing. *What was that about?* You wonder, suddenly you feel really self-conscious; other people are staring at you to, most of them snickering. You hurry to class, hoping you'll disappear by the time you get there. You set your books on your desk, and sink down in your chair. Class is about to start and the teacher steps out of the room to get the last few students from the halls. Some obnoxious kid yells to you from across the classroom, "Hey, did you get dressed in a circus tent this morning?" The class bursts into laughter, and you feel awful; especially knowing that, if it'd been some other kid, you'd have laughed to.

This sort of scenario happens to often, to too many kids. Something needs to happen. Something needs to change. Teachers or principals or school board directors will declare schools, even whole districts, bully free. We all know that's only a title though, because if you pay close enough attention you'll see that bullying still happens. It's in the halls, in the lunchroom, even in the classrooms- right under the teachers' nose. The more that teachers and adults try to stop it, the worse it seems to get, because the more you're NOT supposed to do something, the "cooler" people think it is.

I think it all comes down to the students. If you're one of those kids who just stands back and watches the bullying, even if you don't think it's funny or okay, you could make a huge difference to the bullied kid. You'd be surprised how something as simple as asking them to sit with you at lunch, or standing up for them when they're being bullied could make them feel better, less alone. After all for all you know there could be other kids there who really want to say something, but are afraid to go against the crowd. Seeing you stand up might give them the courage to do the same, but no matter the crowd's reaction, you've just made a difference to the bullied kid.

I think that the only way bulling is ever going to stop is if we, the students, rise up against the bullies and make it known that bullying is NOT WELCOME in our schools. You don't have to be mean to the bullies, because that defeats the purpose, but let it be known that bullying IS NOT COOL, and WILL NOT be tolerated. Let's make our schools TRULY bully-free!

True Happiness

By Joey Nadon

Happiness is found,
In a love so pure
Through hard times,
Happiness is a cure.

Happiness can be found,
In a person, place or thing.
But true happiness
Can't come from everything.

For every person, place or thing ,
Will soon go away,
But true happiness
Will always stay.

It doesn't come from money,
Or clothes or food,
True happiness comes
from a God so good.

He will stay forever,
And never leave your side.
Through the bad and the good
He will help you glide.

Over your troubles
Above your fears,
He will keep you safe
From all your tears.

God brings happiness,
To every person or place.
An everlasting love,
That cannot be replaced.

Come Back

By Miranda Naeem

I have to say I miss you so much!
I think about you every day.
I sit there on the floor crying,
"Why, why, why?"

Why did you leave me?
Please come back.
I'm sitting in my room,
Crying, crying, crying.

This is the time I need you most!
Why did you have to go?
I never got to say goodbye.
I am so sorry for that.

I loved you so much!
I can't stop crying,
I will never forget you.
I just can't.

I love you.

To Write a Story

By: Charlie Nick

You want me to write a story,
to help publish a book,
You want me to entertain an audience,
maybe on how to cook.

I can't write a cook book,
because I'm not a remarkable chef.
I always scorch the food,
I sometimes burn myself.

I could write about band class,
and playing the bassoon,
or reading all the music,
and making a nice tune.

I could write about a sport,
but I'm not the best athlete.
My information would be short,
and not entirely complete.

It would be a good idea to write a how-to book,
about learning to train a dog -
I've had a lot of experience-
I have to play with one all day long!

I am BIG on the environment.
I could write about that,
But there's a lot of information
that I might lack.

I'm capable of writing a novel
With details, pages and such
I have endless ideas
But it might be too much

It might be best to write a memoir,
digging real deep.
But I can't remember much
I'd put my readers to sleep.

I could write a poem,
a story in a rhyming format-
I just wrote one now,
Would you look at that!

Well, I'll just use this story
about choosing what to write
I promise that this poem
Will simply be a delight!!!

Me?

Corey Nierzwick

Why am I such a freak or independent? Lots of people say that I am a freak of nature just from the things I say. But that's not my real personality at home, I am somewhat normal from what I know.

I have odd dreams of dying purple babies and unicorns, my favorite word is meow and I use it at all times. (And at the most random times.) I am obsessed with the Mexican and Asian races, but really I am a little white boy special very special. I have odd secrets that if they got out I would laugh about but really I would be cutting myself on the inside. (But only on the inside).

I don't exactly want to be a freak, but it just comes to me. I am special in my own way, sometimes in my own world. For some reason I can find a way to laugh at nothing in the middle of class and just to have fun.

Most of the time I have a lot of people starring at me wondering what I am doing. I wonder what I am doing too! If I actually did find out I would be like the rest and not understand what I was doing or why I was doing it.

Nobody cares about me. And I over obsess about it. I think you can hear the ocean when you listen to my leg hair.

Friendship

By Emily O'Leary

As I lay in my best friends arms, sobbing and weeping over my grandma's recent death, I think to myself what good friends I have. They are always here for me and never like to see me hurting or sad.

My family just got home only to find my two best friends at my house waiting for me to get home. We had been at my grandma's funeral all day. The last thing I wanted was to have my friends see me like this; all I wanted was to go sit in my bedroom and cry myself to sleep. My friends put their amazing brains together and decided today was not for being sad, it is for being happy that my grandma is not suffering anymore and that she is in a better place. I lay in their arms for about 20 minutes, balling my eyes out, in the blink of an eye, the day gets turned around. We started having fun by playing games, going on a walk, and watching movies. The worst day of my life was just turned into one of the best, thanks to my best friends, that day was just an amazing day.

Today I realized who my true friends were. They showed me that they both care about me and would do anything to make my day. These two girls have been through everything with me from comforting me over my grandma's death to having a great time watching my dad in the Thanksgiving Day Parade. Life is about making choices and when it comes to friends, I am definitely sure I chose the right ones. Since then I have had many hard times and I have needed someone there for me, I just call a friend and I know that they will always be there for me. Friends are like balloons, you keep them very close so they don't fly away, but once you let them go they are gone forever.

Diabetes

By Collin Pavle

It was Friday, February 19, 2011 when I was tested for type 1 diabetes. Diabetes is a disease where your body cannot produce the insulin needed to take sugars from food and use it as energy. After the test my mom and I went home. Around five o'clock the phone rang. Right then, I could see the look on my mom's face and I knew. I had type 1 diabetes.

Without your body producing insulin your blood sugar can get very high. Some symptoms are stomach pains, dry skin and mouth, nausea or throwing up. If your blood sugar gets too high you have a chance of going into diabetic coma. Keeping your blood sugars at a low but not too low number is very important. 150 is a good number, even 200 is considered high.

On the other hand, it is better to have a high blood sugar than a low. If it falls below 70, you can feel a headache, hunger, shaking and weakness. If this happens you should always carry around a high carb snack to get your blood sugar back up. Exercising can bring down your blood sugar rapidly so always carry a snack around.

You're probably wondering how do you eat a meal like breakfast, lunch or dinner? Well, all you need is insulin, a needle and a meter for testing. The meter allows you to check your blood sugar by poking your finger with a tiny needle. You take a small trace of blood and place it onto a strip that connects to a meter. Now, depending on your blood sugar and what you are going to eat, it may vary in how much insulin you have to take.

Diabetes can be very annoying at times, but with it you can still live your daily life. If you don't take care of it, it can lead to blindness, organ failure and foot amputation. Over time you get so used to it, you don't even know you have it. There are a lot of disadvantages but you can also use it as an advantage too.

Slide!

Catie Pelland

As I lift the bat, I shift my weight from foot to foot,
And turn and give the pitcher a fierce look.
I can feel all eyes on me as I stand
My heart starts to race as the ball leaves the pitcher's
hand.
I grip the bat tight as I lean back to swing,
The ball connects with my bat
and makes a noise that sounds like
"Bing!"

I make a clear hit through the sky,
It was going so fast it probably killed a fly.
I start to run as dirt flies into the air from underneath
my cleats.
The ball flies past everyone,
You can feel the heat!
I fly through first, past second, bolt over third,
And slide into home plate!

The team crowds around me and cheers
with a huge smiles on their faces!

Dog Poems

By Josh Perkin

My dogs name is Cisco,
It rhymes with Disco!
He is a beagle,
Which rhymes with Seagull!

He won't let us clip his claws,
But it is probably because he hates
When we touch his paws.

He is scared of a lot of stuff,
But he is very tough.
He is very protective,
Although not exactly like a dog detective.

My other dog's name is Citrix,
It almost rhymes with Matrix.
She is also a beagle,
Which also rhymes with Eagle.

She will let us clip her claws,
Without much of a fight.
Sometimes she'll bark at something,
that isn't in sight.

She is overweight,
But we never let her eat
off the dinner plate.

Simple Text Message

By Alex Peshchanitsky

Simply a text message.
5am at the hospital,
Just killed somebody.
A simple text message,
Ruined your life and someone else's.
Car ruined,
Need money.
The feeling that you killed a person will never go away.
Horrible, terrible feelings.
Should have been the person killed.
Just remember -
Its only one simple text message,
That killed the spirit in you.

By Blood.

By Nick Pham

I just wanted to let you know, that when you tried to take your own life, you were taking out pieces of mine, memories of mine, taking my sister away. Someone to look up to, someone to talk to, someone to give me the best advice. But when I needed you most, you put yourself into a hospital bed.

Unresponsive.

Unreal.

I'm not saying you have to take all of the blame. But our relationship will never be the same. Now I have to deal with this in my own way, trying to get through it, as you're standing completely changed. It's as if I have to walk on glass around you, because you just aren't the same. But I'm different now, too. You've got through it, you're better, but what am I supposed to do? I suppose I'll move on, get over that bump, and I still love you with all that I've got, because you're my sister, depressed or not.

What If

Dedicated to KaSandra

What if there was no light,
nothing wrong, nothing right?
What if you decided,
that you don't want me by your side,
to save me the sight to see you cry?

What if I could save your life,
from this cancer causing you strife?
What if you could turn 11,
and grow to be 77?
What if you could get married,
and start a family?

What if cancer was a lie,
and you were really fine?
What if there was no time,
for you to say good bye?

What if you didn't die,
so your little brother didn't have to wonder why?
What if you were still alive,
so your mother didn't have to cry?
What if you were to know,
how dear we wished you were still here,

What If.

Rainbow After a Storm

By Brooke Plautz

Have you ever thought your life was falling apart, when in reality you have it better then a lot of other people? To be honest that's me. My story is like a rainbow after a storm. Something good always comes out of it. At times it would be a relief if I just took one step back.

I have gone through a lot like, my uncle in the hospital for cancer, my papa just starting chemo and to top it all off drama between friends. I'm always asking "why me" or "does it ever end." People with big homes, lots of money, expensive clothes try to explain how rough the world there are living in is, but they haven't heard my story yet. My parents aren't divorced, that doesn't mean they never fight.

When I'm at school my mind is drifting from school work to what happened through friends and me last week to a blank stare at the teacher. It makes me crazy at every little thing. My peers tell me I wear my heart on my sleeve, meaning I'm an emotional wreck.

Then good things pop up here and there like getting on the all A and B honor roll, or finally getting a good grade on a simple math test and staying fit by being on track. This is where I need to let all the good things roll in and not worry about everyone but me.

Sometimes I've never seen it so clear. Over all the bad, I have realized that I have a loving family, a roof over my head, the greatest friends and I have more then I ever asked for.

Under the Bed

By: Alicia Polk

Flip flop, flip flop. "Oh, here comes the phone!" Can't she see that she threw it in the wrong direction? Who would want to be down here anyway? Dark and cold, who knows how many texts she'll get before she finds this thing? I mean, she's forgotten about me for the past two years! But oh, I'm just that old sock under the bed. Everyone forgets about me!

Seven minutes later… Oh, here she comes, hmm what is she eating? An apple, a piece of chocolate? Oh, it's a piece of ice? What a freak that girl is, I tell you! Why do I even miss her big feet in me? Hmm, what is she saying? Oh, where's your phone? Well darling, it's down here! Right next to me, and I bet you won't find it for a while. Haha, too bad for you!

Oh dear, here comes the little brother, "Alicia, where is my dang phone charger? You always take my stuff without asking, I'm sick of it! Get your own stuff!" Alicia answered back "Get out of my room! Can't you see I'm busy here?" Then, she had a brilliant idea, "Maybe it's in the freezer!" PLOP! I cannot believe you Alicia. Your fourteen and you fall off of a chair? What is wrong with you child?

Obviously, she didn't find it in there! Oh well. When will she ever learn not to throw her stuff around, especially the stuff that means a lot to her? Also, maybe she could clean her room every once in awhile! That's just a thought. I mean, I'm just a sock. What do I know?

Scared Like Crazy

By Edwin Prado

People crying, scared like crazy.
Some confused, people with guns.
Shooting everywhere,
injuries, instant death.

Going to Mexico, a long way to go.
So much violence!
Mexican army, after gang people.
Can't catch them!

Stuffed in the car, hoping to survive.
A nightmare, the worst, a man with a gun.
This trip is the opposite of fun!
I wish it was over.

When the car finally moved
and we found a hotel the nightmare was over.
I tried to sleep on my sisters shoulder.
We all felt relieved, as we all fell asleep.

Just a Game

By Nick Przybylowicz

Football was just a game to me. I played when I was young; but this year was different.

The first day of full pads and hitting was fun! We did blocking drills and we had no center so, my coach looked at me and said, "You, Chevy - you are going to try center." Everyone was laughing because I was 108 pounds and everyone else was at least 160. Even the quarterback was weighed more then me.

Later I was talking to my coach. Who is possibly the nicest guy I've ever met. I asked him, "Why did you put me at a big guy position?"

He looked at me and said, "Chevy, you don't stop fighting there and we need someone like that at center."

I guess that just got me convinced that I could play against some of the bigger kids. The following week I got moved to nose guard. I guess I did pretty well at center. I asked Coach Hale why he put me there he said, "I could see by what you did at center that you could play nose guard."

This season changed my life because my coach helped me be a better person and a better football player.

Global Warming

By Kurtis Reininger

Global warming is bad, yet we can't stop what we have done so far. But, we can prevent it from happening. Global warming will make a global climate shift and will melt the polar ice caps. Icebergs will melt and will raise the water levels and cities will flood around the world. It will disrupt the food chain and most of the population will die. It is imperative that we stop global warming. We need to help the food chain from being disrupted. We can help by driving cars that don't disrupt then ozone layer so much - we need to start driving eco friendly cars.

Most of the species of earth will die if we allow the earth to continue down this path. The dominant species will be the sea animals. Global warming is a serious subject. It could even be tomorrow! We need to stop it as soon as we can. The effects of global worming are deadly. It could be the end of mankind. Some have predicted as soon as 2012. Global warming is happening, if we don't start to help stop its progression we will put mankind in jeopardy. The world will be over run with water and the sea mammals will be the only ones left. If we do not do something soon it will put these same problems on the next generation.

Global warming can kill all of us. Many people don't believe that global warming will be the end of earth as we know it. Global warming will melt the ice caps and the icebergs it will make the water levels rise and will kill most of us. This problem belongs to us, it is up to us to take action NOW to solve it and not leave it to our grandchildren.

My Friends

By Katelyn Rhue

There for me through thick or thin,
Always happy and filling in.
Hanging out and having fun,
We always hate when it's done.
Laughing, playing, joking and more,
Watching movies filled with gore.
Summer comes and summer ends,
And then school eventually begins.
Friends stay and friends go,
Friends are friends where ever they go.
Friends of mine and friends of yours,
We all hang out and everyone knows,
We are friends till the end.
No matter thick or thin.

Family Reunion

By Macey Ronquillo

Every year I look forward to the weekend of my family reunion in Stockbridge, MI. The weekend usually consists of four wheeling, swimming, s'mores, fishing and getting lost in the woods. Last summer the family reunion had to be one of the best ones yet!

Before we leave the night before me and my cousin Emily spend the night at my grandma and grandpa Sparks' house. We pack up their trailer and get our beds ready for the weekend. We can barely sleep that night we stay up and talk about all of the fun we are going to have for the next four days. When we wake up in the morning we load the last of our stuff into the back of my grandma's car. As soon as my grandma and my Aunt Elizabeth (finally) get ready we all pile into the car and complain our heads off about how mushed we are for the next two ours. On the way there we stop at least six times for food, bathroom breaks, and the items that we forgot at home.

Seeing the gigantic Walmart sign as we pull of he interstate makes every single one of us sigh with relief, that sign means only twenty minutes left of being smashed! But first we always stop at Walmart and load up on all the groceries we need for the weekend. We buy lots of food but being with my grandma she buys us a lot of water rafts, sunscreen, bug spray, blankets, coloring books, sand toys and sometimes new swimsuits. Eventually we make our way out of the store, fight over shot gun, get McDonalds (again), and fill up on gas.

On the way to my Papa Mac's property we drive through the smallest towns I've ever seen. We also drive through miles and miles of nothing but corn fields! When we turn down M-36 we start to see left over sparks in the park signs from the year before tied up with shiny blue, silver and red balloons. When we finally arrive at his gate, we start to unbuckle and get excited. When my grandma drives through the opening my other cousins come running from whatever they were doing and rush up to our car. Of course, when my grandma stops the car we only think of getting out and throwing on our nothing suits and jumping in the pond. But first we have to help unpack and finish cleaning the trailer!

When we finally get done doing all our chores it's usually around 6:30, sevenish. It's dark then, but that doesn't stop us from swimming in the pond. My aunts and uncles will turn their cars onto the pond and turn on their headlights so we can swim. When everyone is ready to swim we play Rock, Paper, Scissors to see who gets in first. The first person goes then the rest of us just follow. The pond is usually freezing but it doesn't stop us from climbing on the blowup mountain and jumping on and off the dock/raft. We usually swim until one of the adults tells us to get out, but it doesn't really bother us because we know that what we do next is lots of fun too!

When we get out of the pond we run as fast as we can to our trailers, hop into warm showers and change into our pajamas. When my cousin Emily and I are ready we grab the snack bag and go over to the almost fifteen foot bon fire. There we have a table set up full of graham crackers, marshmallows, chocolate bars, hotdogs, hot dog buns, and a thermos of hot cocoa. When the whole table is gone, we will all slowly start to head for our trailers. Even though we are inside we still have a lot of fun. When we start to yawn and complain about being exhausted, my grandparents make us go to bed and dream about the next four days.

The next day we wake up and are greeted by my grandma's smiles, big hugs and gigantic stacks of chocolate chip pancakes! My grandma tells us the weather for the day and makes sure we have sunscreen and bug spray on before we head outside. In the morning the pond isn't warm enough to swim in yet, so we argue over the four wheelers and who gets to drive them first. When we are done driving, get called back or run out of gas, we are sweating bullets and can't wait to jump in the pond. When it is brighter out the pond is even more fun. We play games as we jump off the dock and see who can stay on the raft the longest.

Later in the evening more of my cousins begin to arrive. That night is full of men doing heavy chores and the women cleaning and cooking the next meal. Finally when everyone is done doing chores and errands my Papa Mac builds another enormous fire and sets up another table full of snacks. That night we go to bed a lot quicker and get up a lot earlier. We wake up to the smell of bacon and pancakes being made at my Aunt Kate and Uncle Gary's trailer. The whole day we spend just like the one before, but we swim a lot more and do more four wheeling.

The last two days my extended family shows up and we do the same things we did the previous two days, except, there are more people to see who can stay on the mountain and raft the longest. When Monday comes that is when we all start to jam the most fun into the day. Monday night we have the biggest bonfire of the weekend and stay up the latest. That night my cousin Emily and I stay up talking about all the stuff we did and how we can't wait for the next year. Tuesday morning we drive the four wheelers into the barn out back and deflate all the floaties and the giant blue mountain. We load all of our stuff into the car and drive two hours home wishing we could have stayed longer.

Every time I go up to my Papa Mac's property I always have a lot of fun. I love spending time with my cousins and with my family that I only see twice a year. I love swimming in the pond, four wheeling through mud puddles and going for late night walks through the woods creeping out my little cousins. Every year I get so excited to go up there but I never want to come home.

Mom

By Alena Sauro

The clock is ticking,
You've been gone for awhile.
You could be anywhere,
a second away or maybe a mile.
Sometimes worrying, waiting,
is the worst part.
Not knowing where you`ve been,
where your heading hurts the heart.

The whole time you're gone,
every little thing I do,
makes me stop and think of you.
The moments pass slowly,
with your questionable acts,
sooner or later,
someone needs to tell me the facts.

Eventually it`s no longer a worry,
it`s just knowing you really don`t care.
Letting the addiction control your life,
seems like your forgetting to be a mother
and a wife.

Biking

By Jenny Schermerhorn

Laying against a tree for me, a road bike!
Come ride me!

Voices, laughing, wait what's that? Footsteps near
There on their way!

I can hardly stand it,
Shouting and yelling for her to see
How much I want to be free.

Yes, finally, okay!
There here, there here, ready to go
Let's ride together as a family!

Pedal, pedal, glide, glide
Up and down those rolling hills
With the wind in her hair.

Going fast, then slow, fast, then slow
As we travel around the camp
Then the town, the four of us.

Going faster than the speed of light
We enter the campground.

Laughing, goofing off, and not paying attention,
Her foot slipped off the peddle and cut her heel.

Dark, dark, red blood dripped down
Her heel going into her shoe.

Rushing her to the foot fountain
Mom on one and me on the other.

We all did our part to help her get better,
I will wait patiently,
For our next ride
Together we will fly!

Madness at Megadeth

By Tyler Schmidt

The concert was insane! We were at DTE Energy Music Theatre. We were on the hill. I was moshing and head banging, until I heard my sister trying to get my attention. I couldn't understand what she was saying at first cause the music was so loud. Then I looked at my dad staring this guy down, my sister was pointing toward the guy when she was talking to me. Then I had it all figured out.

This weird guy who looked like he was in his late 20's, he was drunk and had a beard, was getting closer and closer to my sister and "accidently" bumped into her earlier. So my dad was keeping a close eye on him just to make sure he stays away. Then everything went downhill from there, literally.

The guy came up to my sister again and got extremely to close to my sister, like in her face. So my dad ran over to her and threw him down the hill and he rolled completely down the hill running into to people on the way down. My dad was going to chase him down and start beating on him but my uncle stopped him from doing anything else.

So as the guy was rolling down the hill, my sister was relieved, my uncle was calming my dad down, my dad was a little mad, and I was laughing really hard. That night was crazy and one of the best nights of my life.

How My Life Was Saved

By Katie Schooley

Six years ago, when I was around seven years old, I was diagnosed with scoliosis. Scoliosis is the curvature of the spine. Throughout the years, my spine gradually got worse and worse. My spine looked like a backwards S. We knew we had to do something about it, and fast.

My doctor decided to give me a plastic back brace to wear around my torso area. It was going to try to stop my spine from curving. I wore it from fourth grade through the end of sixth grade. But sadly, it didn't help, at all. When I found out the back brace didn't help, I was informed with some life changing news. I had to have major back surgery.

Almost two years ago, I had the surgery on July 21st, 2009, at Beaumont Hospital. I'm not really sure how to explain what the surgery was like from my point of view, but it was a spinal fusion. Doctors were to fuse two metal rods to my spine and screw them in, and it was going to straighten out my back. That sounded pretty horrific to me. When I look back at the time it happened, it always reminds me of how terrified I was. I remember thinking I was going to get out of the surgery and I would never be the same person again, and that I'd be different from everyone.

It took me about three months to fully recover. It pretty much took over my entire summer that year. But

I feel so blessed, because if I wouldn't have gotten the surgery, sometime in my twenties, I could have possibly died. My spine would have gotten so badly curved, that it would crush my organs, such as my heart, lungs, kidneys, etc. But look at me now, two years later. I don't have to deal with that stupid back brace anymore, I have a perfectly straight spine, and I don't have to worry about the thought of maybe dying because of this. It sucks sometimes having a metal rod in my back. Sometimes I can't bend down, and my back aches so terribly that I have to leave school some days, but I'm happy knowing the fact that that's the pain that saved my life.

The Finals

By Marc Schumacher

Its 7:20 it is the finals at the Ice house. The score is 0 to 0 we are against the Bull dogs. The puck has dropped and the Bull dogs won the face off and then Josh came in and railed the guy then he shot it was a save then the play stopped. The line is me, Josh and Pj the Defensive line is Alex and Jake for my line. We won the face off and passed it back to Pj and he got a break away and scored a top shelf.

Now the score is 0 to 1 and 3:00 min left in the 1st period but then I got a break away decked then scored. On the right side 0 to 2 with 1:22 sec left in the period. But when there was about 30 sec left they scored and the period is over. The 2nd period hit with a nice goal and the score is 1 to 3 it is the 3rd period the Bull dogs have a break away and scored and it is 2 to 3.

The first line is out again then Dan was on a break away then mist a little on the left and the other team retrieved the puck. Then the player past our defense and scored so now it is tied 3 to 3 and it is now overtime. I started he faceoff and past it back to Alex and he made a good shot but it went high and mist to behind the net. But then Josh took the puck and slide it up then shot a top shelf goal. The game ended 3 to 4.

Mourning

By Molly Seelig

Sun shining, stars on the ground
Hollywood Blvd., I'm looking around

Fighting tears of my grandfather's death
The love, the loss, I take in a breath

People who hope their dreams have started
Carrying their instrument; they step into the city full
hearted

A day ago my family and I went to his memorial
Hearing other people say his name feels very
territorial

While others thought their talent was supreme
Now sot on the ground with a lost dream

Memories of fishing on Canadian Lakes
We tubed a lot and made many mistakes

Taking pictures in front of Gruamen's Chinese
Theater,
and walking for miles
My family and I were full of smiles

When I think about his funeral the memories flow
The fear, the sadness, with good things in tow
Whenever I think about him now my feelings grow

In Loving Memory:
Grandpa Seelig
1940-2010

Flying Dream

By: Blanca Serna

Well, when I was about five years I wrote to Santa that I wanted to be able to fly. That's what I wanted for Christmas. On Dec. 24th I went to sleep right away. The very next day I woke up really early, and I went to my mom's room. I got on top of her bed, stood up straight, and jumped off. My mom just heard a big collapse. She went running right away to the room. I was on the floor crying. She said, "Honey, what were you thinking?"

I said, "I wanted to be able to fly like the people on TV."

She said, "The people on TV really can't fly at all."

I thought she was lying.

So that same year we went to Mexico for a family vacation. We went to visit my grandmother. She had a really big house, and a really big roof. She also had this really pretty big umbrella. One day I had this great idea. I ran back down stairs, got the umbrella. I climbed back up the stairs, and I got on top of the roof. I open the umbrella took a big deep breath, and I jumped off.

I was on the floor crying when my mom came running. She said once again, "Honey what were you thinking?"

I said, "I just want to be able to fly in the sky."

She said, "You know the people on TV can't really fly it's all just made up."

I was really disappointed; I really wanted my flying dream to come true. Until this day I still want to be able to fly. I want to feel, how it feels to be able to fly around the sky. But one day my dream will come true. Even if I fall or sky dive through the air - that will make my dream still come true.

A Painful Day

Marcos Serrano

I can't believe this! It's the day before Thanksgiving, and it is eleven o'clock at night, and I'm on my way to the hospital! Here I am walking in with my good friend Nick, and my Mom, and this pain on my shoulder is ridiculous. I think it's pretty dumb they won't let my friend, Nick come into the back of the hospital with me. He is practically like family.

Ugh, are you serious? Why are these stupid doctors taking so long? Oh, here he is after like half an hour! Why is he asking all of these dumb questions? I already told him that it's my shoulder that hurts. I am starting to think this isn't a real hospital.

OUCH! Why did you just take my shirt off like that? You could've just cut it off, that really hurt.

These doctors are stupid! My mom tells them I am allergic to codeine, and what do they do? They give me codeine. It wasn't such a big deal because my heart just calmed it's self down. Finally, I am getting my x-rays. But, of course, I end up waiting another half an hour. Here comes the x-ray doctor. How come she tells me to hold up my hurt shoulder so she can take the pictures? That pain was horrible. After that they tell us to wait in the back for the results which took about forever. And what is really funny is they tell me my collar bone is broken! Which I already knew! And to top it all off they 'accidently' threw my shirt away. So I am going home shirtless in November!

Yes, we are finally going to leave the hospital. Before I leave they put on my brace, and my sling. They accidently hit my collar bone! Ugh! Some hospital!

Death in Disguise

By Mitchell Shedlowsky

It's a cold gray day,
Matching my feelings,
And my dog has been having fun,
In a forest by a lake.

For him we gave,
In all his life,
The very best day,
That we could ever make.

We are all sad,
When we get back home,
And he wants to play more,
As a truck comes, emotions rise.

My dog jumps in,
He doesn't know,
That the truck,
Is death in disguise.

A Real Best Friend

By Naomi Smith

She didn't know that her butt was wet,
But when I told her she started to sweat.

She threw on some sweatpants and started to run,
Somehow I knew that this week would be fun.

She swore on her life that she didn't pee,
But I didn't know how else this could be.

Then I remembered my water jug spill,
Now it was me she was ready to kill.

Inside the bathroom was lots of hair stuff,
Like hairspray and mouse to make your hair fluff.

So I got on my knees and grabbed a blow-dryer,
The heat was on low so I turned it up higher.

She looked at me and gave me a smirk,
We never believed this would actually work.

Her shorts finished drying with minutes to spare,
Even if they hadn't we wouldn't have cared.

This is how I know that she's my best friend,
Since I would never blow-dry anyone else's rear-end!

The Circle

By Nash Soderberg

Sleeping giant,
Beginning to wake,
Eternal sleep,
About to break,

Stretching limbs,
Bare to the skin,
Spinning the clothing,
Of it's own kin,

Bright blanket of green,
The clothing he created,
To his great surprise,
Was being invaded,

These creatures were small,
All sizes and colors,
All making nests,
They were fathers and mothers,

They did not hurt the giant,
They weren't harmful at all,
They just sought the protection,
Of the giant tall,

The next creature,
Wasn't as so,
He brought out machines,
He wanted Giant to go,

Machines began to cut,
Giant's legs broke,
What lay in front of the man?
A lumbering oak,

The creatures inside,
They flew away,
From their families and homes,
They knew they couldn't stay,

Giant was cut,
From head to toe,
The man didn't care,
He caused so much woe,

Giant began to bleed,
His kinds' own blood,
What   we   call   sap,
While he lays in the mud,

The pieces of Giant,
Were thrown into fire,
Giant's resting place,
His funeral pyre,

Dear Adult World!

I do not understand why adults always think that kids are bad! I mean, yeah, we do bad things sometimes, but not terrible! Let me tell you, we have to make mistakes that's how we learn. You made them too!

Here's an example: My friends and I were just hanging out by 7-11 without causing trouble. We weren't expecting to be getting yelled at by people. We were just sitting on the sidewalk, chilling and texting or talking on our phones. We weren't bothering anyone. When all of the sudden, this lady gets out of her car and starts yelling at us! Saying we should have better things to do. So, my friend asks her why is it any of her business what we do?

Of course then she thinks we were being smart mouths. (We were kind of laughing when she walked up to us because she had two huge Big Gulps in her hands. We thought that it was pretty funny to carry those with you just to yell at some kids. How about if you leave them in the car?) So after she was done yelling at us she went into 7-11 told the manager. In addition, she came back out, got into her car, got on her phone and called the police! Seriously! She told us to wait there. So, we did.

We were there for about 20 minutes and finally the police came. She was telling the policemen what happened. The best was the he yelled at her for calling the police when it was not being an emergency!

So, please adults trust us kids, maybe just a little, when we are just sitting there.
Sincerely,

Tyler Spencer

Madison

By Nicole Stanisz

She has long blond hair,
And two bright blue eyes.
She is one beautiful girl
And that, that is no lie.

She's a star in the making,
There's so much she can do.
I know that I can always say,
"Maddie, I'm proud of you."

She can always make me laugh,
Even when I cry.
She comforts me with all her love,
Cause there's a big supply.

As all this time flew by,
She has never left my side.
Through all the things that we've been through,
Our friendship never died.

These memories, they pile up
Every time we're together.
I love her, she loves me
We're Best Friends Forever.

Birthday Dinner

Nick Sumner

It was my favorite weekend of the year, my birthday weekend. I was going to dinner with my family; because it's my aunt's birthday too. We both decided to go to Red Lobster for our dinner. I invited a friend over so I wouldn't be alone; and have someone to talk too. We were all getting ready to go to dinner; and being able to see our family.

We arrived at the restaurant and everyone got out of there cars and started to walk towards the restaurant. My friend kept telling me to prank my mom or dad, but I didn't really want to. After awhile they sat us down at our table. The waitress ordered our drinks and appetizers. She came back and handed us our drinks and straws.

When I looked over to pick up my straw for my drink; I saw a straw with a sealed end. I showed my friend and he told me to prank my mom. I thought about it for awhile and decided to do it. So while she was talking to my aunt; I took her straw out and put the sealed straw in; with the sealed side down so she wouldn't notice. The straw kept popping up. I was afraid I was going to get caught but she never looked back; I finally got the straw to stay down. I couldn't wait to see her try to drink it.

My dad, my friend, and I were waiting for her to

try to take a drink. We were all laughing just thinking about it. Finally she started to turn to take a drink. My dad, my friend, and I all calmed down for the moment. She went to take a drink and nothing came out; she looked at the straw puzzled, and tried again. My dad, my friend, and I were all laughing extremely hard; she looked at us and said "Why are you laughing so hard what's so funny?" I told her that my dad said a joke and she believed it. She tried to take another drink; her face turned a dark red and looked like a puffer fish.

She looked at us and "said what did you do" I said, "look at your straw;" she pulled out the sealed straw and got very angry. We were all laughing and didn't care what she said; it was hilarious. Everyone else looked over and saw what happened and started laughing. Even my mom changed her mood and started to laugh a little. It was my favorite, and best weekend I had ever had. I can't wait to have my birthday weekend next year; but it still won't be even close to this one.

Worst Day Ever

By Nichole Sutton

It's a beautiful, summer day in 2002. I'm 5 years old, running around in the grass in my yard with my best friend Erdem. My bright pink Barbie Jeep is parked in my garage. We have nothing better to do besides go for a ride in it. We hop in the purple, plastic seats; I was in the passenger side, Erdem was driving. We back out of the hot, black, slightly crackled driveway and go to the right, where there is a dead end where we would turn around.

As we progress down the street, the car begins to lose speed slowly but surely and we decide to return back to my house early. We turn into a nearby neighbor's driveway. The moment Erdem presses the reverse button, a raging black Labrador jolts out of from the side of the brick house, raging more than a fat lady that got her Twinkie stolen by a seagull. It thrashes and rips a chunk out of my right arm and it oozes dark red blood. I was bawling my eyes out so we abandon the Jeep and run back to my house. When we arrive I run inside and tell my mom about what happened as Erdem goes back to bring back my Jeep, after all it was only about 3 houses over.

As I'm wiping the blood off of my arm, animal control comes and tells my mom that if this happens again they will "put it to sleep" although she doesn't tell me that. Instead she tells me they would just lock it in a little bird cage, at the time I believe this though. I'm terrified of dogs, and I never ever want to look at one again.

Now fast forward to the year 2011. I'm over my fear of dogs. They aren't all the same vicious animals as the dog that tore my arm up so many years ago. I am not afraid.

Sk8ing vs. Biking

By Dillon Talbot

Everybody thinks that biking is better than skateboarding, which it really isn't. You can do more and cooler tricks on a skateboard. You can do kick flips and heel flips. However, you can't do any flips on a bike besides front and back flips.

What really irritates me is that people really think that biking is better than skateboarding. Skateboarding has more sponsorships and it is more popular, but biking is catching up to skateboarding.

Snowboarding is also better than skiing. It's just that snowboarding is just like skateboarding but skiing is not like biking. It's just not as cool as snowboarding and skateboarding. I guess that means that skateboarding is better than biking!

Dear Readers,

We just got back from Islands of Adventure. We are now at our hotel and I'm soaked! We went on this ride called Toon Lagoon. It is a boat and the whole ride is on water. The wait was an hour long and boring. The line was crammed in to one little room that had ramps all the way down to where you were loaded on to the ride. Anyway, when we were finally seated, my grandma, mom, brother, and had to get in these tiny little seats with no leg room at all. The ride was going like 5 mph, and I thought I might have been waiting an hour just to go on a kiddy ride. The ride just kept on going up, and down, these little bumps. Suddenly we swept into a cave and before we knew what was happening we shoot down a hill, extremely fast! The only thing I saw was water, heart pounding, I knew I was doomed, so I just closed my eyes. When I opened them my sunglasses, shirt, shorts, and even my shoes were drenched with water! When we got off the soaking ride, we had to walk through a maze, to find our way out. I looked at the rest of my family. Dry! They had like a drop on them! Me, I was soaked! My shoes were squeaking with each step. My shirt was stuck to my body, and my shorts were so heavy I had to hold them up! I guess that's what I get for sitting in the front. Then we finally went to go find my dad. He was too much of a wimp to get wet and had decided not to go on the ride. On the way to find him, there was a huge dryer. It reminded me of a giant dog house with hot air blowing out. I tried my best to dry off, but it didn't work so well. The only part of my body that got dry was my shoes. The ride was fun except for the part where you get drenched with water!

So readers are warned you will wait endlessly to ride Toon Lagoon. It will be a cramped ride with a slow start. But you MAY GET SOAKED, so beware!

By Seth Terry

My Life

By: Christina Thompson

For the last fourteen years. At my dad's house, my life has been horrible! I'm tired of it; he's been treating me like a maid. Making me cook dinner every night for the entire family, clean the whole house, and usually he won't let me hangout with my friends.

At my dad's house there used to be chores for everyone; but for the last three years there hasn't been. We had chores, and one day my dad stopped paying us, so my brother and sister stopped cleaning. He stopped paying us because he started running out of money and needed to save some for the bills. Somehow I got stuck doing all the work in the house because I hate it being dirty. When the house is dirty it makes me feel like I'm sick. Plus, my dad rarely cooks so I have to do that too otherwise we would have fast-food everyday. My dad might clean something up every three months, and that makes me feel even more like an unpaid maid.

If I moved to my mom's house I think things would be very different like they were in the summer. In the summer I don't have to do anything. My mom does all the cooking and cleaning in the house. I like being there because it gives me time off from my horrible life. Plus she lets me see and talk to my friends. My mom actually talks to me and does stuff with me. That's makes me feel like a normal kid not an adult .The only thing I worry about is that I might eventually have to do the same stuff there as I do at my dads. Or, she might treat me different when my brother comes to stay. Or maybe if it was a permanent move not just a visit in the summer.

The Zip Line

By Justin Torres

One day over the summer I was very bored and had nothing to do. As I was sitting outside I noticed my older brother matt walking towards me with a long line of rope in his arms and a big grin on his face and said to me "were going to make a zip line". So I said to him "ok, how are we going to do that?" And matt said "you'll see just go get Branden, Chris and Jacob so they cam help". I was just thinking wow this is going to be funny to watch I just know some ones going to get hurt.

After I got the rest of my brothers to help we walked around the yard to look for the perfect spot to make it. Then we found the perfect spot to put the zip line. It would start at the top of this really tall tree in my front yard ending at the gate leading in to my back yard. After spending a half hour on it we finally finished. The only problem was that nobody wanted to go down it. Then my brother matt grabbed an old belt climbed up the tree and slid down the zip line. Everyone figured that if he went down it we could go down it so we all went down taking turns.

Then my brother matt wanted to go again but he wanted to put the rope up higher so he did. My brothers and I told not to do it that it was a bad idea but he didn't care what we said and still did it any ways. As he just left the tree and started to slide down the rope the belt he was sliding down the rope with snapped in half and matt fell of the rope and smacked his back on the ground and my brothers and I just busted out with laughter. After matt got up he started laughing too. The five of us had such a great time that day I think that was one of my favorite days that summer.

Basketball

By Jordan Tower

Offense
Dribble, Lay-up
Running, Passing, Shooting
Team, Friends, Ball, Game
Moving, Stealing, Helping
Intercept, Shuffle
Defense

I don't play racquetball, I play basketball
I'm not interested with a ball and a wall, I like a hoop
and a ball
My love for the game, is more than all the fame
It's not about making money on the spot; it's all about
making the shot
If I had a choice, to play sports or have a voice
I'd rather walk, then talk
Id chose sports any day; they're extremely fun to play
For some you have to pay, but it's worth it to play
Basketball is the best sport; I'm always ballin on the
court
You can be tall or short, and still good at the sport
This is why I play basketball, and not racquetball
I'd rather dribble a ball, then hit it against a wall

The Hatchet Incident

By: Chris Wakefield

It was the summer of '02, June 16 to be exact; me, my dad and some other people from our church where camping at Fox Lake Farms for the yearly father son campout. My dad and some of his friends went out on the lake to fish and left me with Mr. Lee, who is a registered paramedic and although the teacher at Lees Martial Arts, his son Caleb and my friend James Thomason and as I was walking around I noticed that we had a small wood pile so being eager to help around camp I thought "hey, maybe I can help by cutting more wood" and then I thought "wait what will I cut the wood with; oh wait didn't dad bring the hatchet all I have to do is just go to the car, get the hatchet and cut some wood" now I don't know who's bright idea it was to keep a hatchet in the reach of a seven year old but when I got it I remembered a small tree next to the lake cabin that would be easy to cut down. When I got to the tree I just stood in front of it for a second then I just started hacking at it and lucky for me the blade was a little dull but unlucky for me I swung as hard as I could, missed the tree and the bottom point, the sharpest point on the hatchet, went right into my shin causing immense pain and after just laying there bleeding Mr. Lee heard me and went to get his EMT bag. When my dad got back he was furious at me for taking the hatchet and slicing my leg open. He acted as if I purposely stuck the hatchet in my leg after about ten minutes he bandaged my leg and told my dad that I wouldn't have to have stitches but I would have to go home and not do anything for a couple of weeks, which is sort of my specialty now, so for three weeks I was in excruciating pain but at least I didn't need stitches. And even to this day nobody trusts me with a ax or hatchet, which is very annoying at some times.

The Almost Surviving Survivors

By Jared Wolfe

"People, people calm down." Tyler yelled over the crowd of survivors. "I know our food and water supplies are running low but we hopefully have enough to make it to Atlanta. The zombie horde that's following us consists of about five hundred from most of the cities and towns where we saved you from. There starting to catch up to us, even though were only twenty miles away, we're going to have to take up a defense position in the next city or town we come pass".

As he looked over the barren landscape of a destroyed city and decided that they would take position in the still standing buildings. "We're taking up position here. Get anything you can and put up barriers in any entrance that a zombie would be able to get in through" Tyler told the survivors. Everyone rushed to get the buildings boarded up. "Phyllis, get your brother and come back to me" Tyler said.

Once Phyllis got his brother and came back. " can you two see if you can find any food or water, also anything that could go as a weapon in case our ammo runs out" Tyler asked. "We sure can Tyler" Phyllis said as they rushed to go look for food and water.

Phyllis and John handed any big metal scraps to the other survivors to use on the buildings. They found some canned food and some salty snacks in a destroyed grocery store. The y packed it into whatever bag or backpack they found or the other survivors had brought over. Phyllis found some water leaking from a pipe going to some of the buildings being boarded up. He got water bottles and buckets to get the water. After Phyllis had gotten all the water from the pipes John took out the loose pipes to go as a weapon.

When Phyllis and John returned to Tyler with the leftover food and water that wasn't given to the survivors. "We gave all that we could to the other survivors" John said. "This is all that's leftover" Tyler asked. "Yes" Phyllis answered. "Good, know go help the other survivors on the buildings.

The survivors were now working on other entrances and second barriers so the zombies would have to go through two barriers and rooms to get to the survivors. Once they had gotten into rooms in the buildings with all their packs and weapons in case the zombies were able to get in. After Tyler looked over the buildings, he went back to his own. Then after a couple minutes passed they were able to hear the zombies coming into the city. The moaning and groaning got louder as the zombies surrounded the building where the survivors were hiding. In one of the buildings there was a crash where the zombies had found a weak spot. Then in the other buildings, the zombies started to climb though open and broken windows to get to the people. Anyone who hadn't been eaten started to make there way to the roof for protection from the on coming zombies.

Once the zombies had gotten to the roof with the survivors, they started to charge at them. The survivors took whatever they could to fight off the zombies, but were soon over powered and eaten alive by the zombies. Now all the zombies were thinking, "What a great lunch, now I want a sandwich."

The Lone Soldier

By Henry Wraight

Boys sent into the unknown
To be tried by the fires of war
And forged into men.

They trained for days
Under the foreign moon,
To learn the skills,
And the weapons,
Of war.

Through dust and fire
Blood and steel,
They became brothers
In all but blood.

Though their enemies were
As determined as they were ruthless,
The boys fought on
Never losing sight of their goal.

But as all things must
Their brotherhood came to an end,
And one was left standing
A lone warrior on a desolate plain.

Though his brothers are gone
He fights on,
To avenge his comrades
And find the peace that eludes him.

And though the battle is over
He fights on
Oblivious to all,
Except the ghosts of the past.

At long last
The fighting is over,
And as he enters the void
He smiles,
For at long last he will see his brothers again.

"It often requires more courage to dare to do right
than to fear to do wrong."
-Abraham Lincoln

Grand Prix

By Madison Wright

I walk across the pool deck and into the small tent that is apparently the ready room. The crowd is already up and cheering as I wait in a small folding chair along with five other girls.

Wait a sec… oh my god you have got to be kidding me! Who is this little girl that just walked into the tent? Is she swimming in this heat? Ha-ha well, we all know who's taking eighth in this race. Just look at her trying to fit in with us, she is so puny and pale with no tattoos and tiny biceps. How is she going to pull herself through the water with those toothpick arms? How did she even make it to the A final? And what has she got draped over those weak shoulders?

Wow! She's using a hotel towel instead of a warm up jacket, and she is barefoot! She is totally new at this or else she would be wearing Nikes and a warm up jacket just like everyone else in this tent. Okay, seriously, how old is this girl? And why does she keep smiling at everybody? Oh, God! I just hope that she doesn't put on a sob show after she loses, that would just be pathetic.

I turn my head to the sudden roar of the crowd outside so it must be time to swim. Good luck puny girl, you're going to need it…

Music

By Mai Nou Yang

Music creates a melody,
    I feel in my heart,
    As soon as it starts.
    Guitar, piano, drums and vocal
        Is something I focal.

        Listening to music makes my heart race.
        Make me feel like I'm in a whole different place.
        Closing my eyes takes the stress out
        I'm completely relived, I have no doubt

The tune of music shows pride,
        Makes me feel happy and want to cry.
        When I turn on the music and start singing
        It calm me down and it is relaxing.

        Hip hop is the music to my motion,
        Dancing express my emotion.
        The drum beat of the melody
        is jumping and thumping.

Overhearing country music,
>   Makes me want to bring out my guitar
>   And start rockin' like a star.
>   This is what I'm passionate for!
>   And I love Music.

The Love Stare

By Katie Ziem

Walking into Comerica Park, I smell hot dogs, nachos, and roasted peanuts. It was a very sunny and mildly hot day, I walked down to our third row seats right behind third base!

***

Today is a great day; the sun is shining. What a terrific day for a home game. I am on the field warming up, before the game. I see and hear a group of people chanting my name! I walk over to the screaming fans.

***

Looking out onto the field, I spot the love of my life; Miguel Cabrera warming up. With his name and number written on my shirt, all I can hope for is for him to sign my ball. Glancing in my direction, I can't believe he's jogging my way!

***

Standing on the edge of the field, I spot this blonde with a Tigers jersey on. The closer I look, the more I can tell that her jersey says my name and my number on it. She begins to walk toward me. I think I'm sweating more than I have in any game before! My signature for other fans' souvenirs is beginning to get a little shaky. I don't think I can contain myself anymore! I just know that she is the one!

***

I will fight this crowd to get over to him even if it is a little difficult. Being short could be an advantage, as well as a disadvantage. I'm on my way to my delicious Mexican, and I make it as far as I can. I see him signing baseball, after baseball. I spot an empty chair which is a great place for standing. Once I climb on the green, steamy plastic chair, I hold out my ball in hopes of him signing it. He looks straight into my eyes, and grabs my ball, his fingers gently rub mine.

***

Seconds after she actually made it to me, I could not help but grasp the ball in her hand first. I take my time signing hers, because I want my signature to look best for my lady. I don't want to hand the ball back to her, because I don't want her to leave. I can tell that she wasn't up for leaving either. I really want to write my phone number on her ball, but my agent wouldn't be happy with it. I hand the ball back to her, and right when I did, she starts to walk away. I couldn't take watching her leave. I would've gotten too emotional, so I couldn't do anything but leave as well.

***

After he signed my ball, he gave it back probably hoping I shouldn't leave. But I thought I should go, so another fan could take my spot. As I stepped off of the chair, he was leaving as well, calmly wiping the tears off his face.